John Alite

MAFIA INTERNATIONAL

Gotti Enforcer for the Gambino Crime Family

LOUIS ROMANO

ISBN: 978-1-944906-35-1
Printed in the U.S.A. First Edition, 2021 Vecchia Publishing

Cover photography by Fadil Berisha

Also By Louis Romano

Acknowledgments

I'd like to thank Louis Romano for taking on this project and getting it completed. His strong commitment and brilliant style of writing makes him second to none.

— John Alite

While writing this book I spent a great deal of time with John Alite, listening to hundreds of his stories on his personal life and his life in organized crime. I am ever grateful John selected me to write his story.

I am also grateful to Anthony Ruggiano, Jr. for revealing to me the history on his father, and their relationship with John Alite.

There are quite a few people with whom I interviewed in gathering information for this book— Italians and Albanians, organized crime members and civilians, all who worked in some way with John during his years with the Gambino crime family. I thank those who contributed to this book whose names I will not expose here.

Kathleen Collins did her usual brilliant job of advising me on the story, editing the book, proofreading, and putting the physical book together.

Special thanks to Bridget Fuchsel for her expert proofreading. Brilliant is not enough of a word to describe her.

— Louis Romano

Dedication

I want to dedicate this book to all my family and friends on the street who died, and to my father who taught me to never quit and to push through to be successful.

To all the young people: The contrast of years living the "high life" compared to "getting life" is vast. Ten or twenty years on the streets is paled by looking at forty-plus years behind bars.

— John Alite

I dedicate this book in a gratitude of thanks to John Alite, to the young people he encourages to live a life free of criminal activity.

— Louis Romano

A Note From the Author

MEETING JOHN

Fortunately for me, I met John Alite several times over lunches and dinners.

The first time was at The River Palm Restaurant in Edgewater, New Jersey. A great, busy spot with fabulous food.

I selected a semi-circular, high-backed leather and rich mahogany appointed booth not far from the long, crowded bar.

To look like a writer, I wore a black golf shirt under a maroon sports jacket and jeans. John came in wearing a tight black leather jacket over a tighter white button-down shirt and black pants. His shirt had the first few buttons opened, exposing his firm, buffed chest and a tattoo that crawled up to his tanned neck.

After ten minutes, I could no longer suck in my gut, and I just let my belly flop over my belt.

We were meeting to discuss a possible role for John in a movie we were planning for my book BESA, which is about the Albanian mob having a war with the New York mafia.

John gave me a rapid-fire soliloquy on the many crimes he committed while in the mafia, the horrific jails he did time at in Brazil, and what led him to cooperate with the federal government.

John recognized someone at the bar and just gave them a cold stare.

At that point, I realized if anyone was going to put a hit on John, I would be shot and killed.

"John, I have to ask you a question."

"Sure, Lou."

"Aren't you ever worried about anyone from the mob, like the Gambinos or someone, walking in and…you know…?"

He flashed his pearl-white teeth and got serious.

"They have to worry about me. I did all the work, and they know what I'm capable of."

At that moment, I knew he was the baddest, toughest, most fearless man I would ever meet in my entire life.

—LOUIS ROMANO

My good friend, ex-FBI, David Gentile. A true gentleman.

Me speaking to troubled youths

John Alite   MAFIA INTERNATIONAL
Gotti Enforcer for the Gambino Crime Family
As Told to Author Louis Romano

This is a riveting, real-life story of John Alite, whose multi-million-dollar heroin and cocaine deals, robberies, savage beatings and murders, and New York mafia street life as a hit man and enforcer for the Gambino crime family expanded into his own worldwide operation. It's all chronicled here, and how that glamorous, yet treacherous life led to John being a man on the run and a man who realized he could never trust anyone except himself. Having been captured numerous times, he'll explain what it was like to be in prisons around the world, sometimes with terrorists, famous people, and well-known gang members, and when it all came crashing down, and he decided to change his life.

Alite has been soundly criticized by some former mob members and others regarding his sincerity with respect to his work with young people.

Alite's focus is to prevent the "kids" from glorifying the mob. They view the mafia from what they see in films and on television and various pod casts and do not understand the evil and treachery which is pervasive in that life.

Following Alite's many lectures at high schools, colleges and institutes, and how he replies and counsels to the hundreds of e-mails he receives from young people, is proof positive of his noble intentions.

John Alite doesn't preach, rather he advises those who want to spend their lives attached to a life of crime and what that will lead to… death or prison, is a credit to his new life.

For those who do not believe Alite's intentions, no proof or explanation will suffice. For those who know John and understand his mission, no explanation is necessary.

Before the age of eight, John Alite rubbed elbows with powerful bosses and made men of the mafia, and he didn't even know it. He was a little boy who looked up to killers and gangsters, knowing at that young age that the life of crime was his calling in life. By the time Alite turned twenty, most of the gangsters whom he knew from childhood were having to answer to him.

The fact that Alite was of Albanian descent in the mostly Italian mob world didn't matter in his daily activities. Except for the mafia rule that disallowed him from becoming a made man, he was the go-to guy in the largest, most powerful mafia family in the United States, the Gambino crime family, and eventually respected around the world. It took a rare talent for anyone to be able to earn millions of dollars, let *alone to have what it takes to be a cold-blooded killer and assassin. Johnny Alite balanced being a good earner and an effective and feared enforcer, which he did extremely well. Alite had grown to be the perfect gangster.*

My life was unrestrained violence twenty-four hours a day, every day I was in the life. I was feared and a force to be reckoned with. The number of men, cartels, law enforcement agencies, or mafia members against me never worried me. I knew I'd be smarter, tougher, crazier, and willing to go so far as to lose my life in order to take things to the highest level possible both in and out of jail.

I had the intelligence and foresight needed to not only survive the streets among dangerous men, but I also had the knowledge and skills and above all, the mindset needed to carry out murders, violence, and any level of crime with cold and lethal precision. Add with that the right connections all over the world, and I couldn't be stopped.

The power, recognition, and respect Alite gained within the Gambino crime family, and every other crime family for that matter, intricately connected him to such arch criminals as Fat Andy Ruggiano; Anthony "Gas Pipe" Cassio; Blacky Charlie Luciano; Tommy Gambino, the son of Carlo Gambino, one of the most famous gangsters ever; Tommy's cousin, Phil Barone, a gold shield detective; Joe Gambino; and many more names that have less notoriety attached to them. But Alite didn't stop there. He was bound and determined to make a name for himself that would be forever recognized and respected in any conversation about the American mafia and to go down in the annals of mafia history as one of the greatest, if not the greatest.

In John Alite's own words: I immersed myself further and further into the matrix of the mafia and beyond. I extended my relationships with other mafia factions across the United States and constructed my own international drug connections. I had associations with drug cartels in over ten countries and a vast network of buyers and sellers across the globe. It was unheard of for one man in the criminal underworld to garner such a complex network, but I did it. And I loved it.

By the late 90s, the structure of Cosa Nostra, the Sicilian Mafia, was deteriorating before my very eyes. It had become disjointed and weak, just like the men running it. As the mafia was falling apart at the seams, I was going rogue, doing what I wanted when I wanted, and no one was able to stop me.

I had become a threat to the mafia on too many levels to count. They didn't like that they could not control me, they didn't like that I was Albanian, and they didn't like that I had acquired such enormous, worldwide control, power, and wealth.

There would be a high price to pay for John going against one of the largest families in organized U.S. crime, and eventually, John would also find himself on the run from the United States government. With a lifetime of murder and racketeering charges to his name, the RICO Act would be closing in on him everywhere he turned. John could feel the vise grip that law enforcement had on him. He painfully had to leave his family and everything he knew and loved behind. Forced into hiding, Alite moved from one country to the next over several continents, just to survive and have another day of freedom.

I was a wanted man, and the governments around the world weren't going to stop until they had me.

What follows is what got John into his horrendous nightmare, his one-way ticket to hell, and what he did about it.

Excerpt from Ronnie "One Arm" Trucchio's 2006 courtroom opening statement about Johnny Alite:

"Johnny Alite is a rogue. He was a loose cannon... There's a careful line you got to walk when you're in the street, because there's enough enemies out there...Because you don't want him one day doing what he does to everybody else. You've got to watch your back."

CHAPTER 1

People wonder if John Alite was a man possessed by his enormous driving ego, pure evil in his heart and soul, or did he have a human side—a conscience?

He casually tells this story.

I was burying the body of a man who I just shot in the head five times when I bolted awake. I ran my hand over my face, wiping away thin beads of sweat from my forehead, reliving the dream of the last murder I committed. My life was getting more dangerous to live with each day that passed. I glanced at the clock. It was two in the morning, and I doubted I could go back to sleep. My mind never stopped flip-flopping from one random thing to the next. It took constant thought to be able to stay a step ahead of everyone and keep the control I needed on the streets. I was constantly thinking and brainstorming about the many businesses I owned, protecting my crew, and who owed me money. Many times throughout the day, I would get a flashback of a beating, shooting, or a murder I committed. The main thought that consumed me the most, however, was making it to the absolute top of the game, and I was willing to do anything to get there."

The combination of fearlessness and his expert use of the element of surprise were just some of the tools Alite possessed that made him so dangerous.

My thoughts wandered to the baseball-bat beating I gave a guy the night before. I had taken a moment to run into one of my drug spots, a well-known bar in Queens, New York, to collect money. When I came out of the bar, I found this guy leaning over the passenger side window of my Corvette, talking to my girl. I gruffly told him to get his hands off my car and to get lost. He sized me up, wearing a cocky grin. I sensed he was thinking he could take me because he was almost twice my build. He said a few terse words, which was his mistake. I had my baseball bat in hand before he could finish his sentence, and I cracked him over the head. He would now know who I was, and every time he would go to a baseball game or get a haircut, he would remember the Louisville Slugger with the Willie Mays name embedded on his skull.

I let out a sigh and rolled out of bed. It was pointless to try to sleep that night. Sometimes, I'd get frustrated for the lack of sleep, but it would soon dissipate—usually get replaced with adrenaline rushes, which could give me energy for days. When I was restless, I found that it was good to take a drive to clear my head.

By this time in my life, I was moving a vast amount of drugs, and I figured I could at least be productive and check in on my stops. I threw on a pair of jeans and t-shirt and then headed for the door, grabbing the keys to my father's Monte Carlo on the way out. It wasn't ordinary for someone to have so many connections at such a young age, but I did. Because I knew so many people from all walks of life, it wouldn't take me long to become one of the main drug suppliers in the city.

The neighborhoods surrounding Alite's home were full of gangs and crews that they referred to as "pockets." Some of those pockets were directly involved with the mafia, and others were directly involved with Alite himself on a very personal and intricate level, especially since he grew up with most of the people involved. The more well-known factions of those gangs were the Crash and Carry Crew, the Bath Avenue Boys, the notorious and violent Giannini Crew, the Youngs Crew, Massa Crew, and the 102 Park Boys. Not only did Alite intimately know those crews, but he also knew hundreds of other crews and guys on the streets from New York to New Jersey and beyond.

Alite was around eighteen years old and in phenomenal shape. His body was ripped; he was training regularly in a boxing gym, running ten to fifteen miles a few days a week, and was as strong as an ox.

As I stepped outside into the cool night, I was already planning my first stop. I cranked up the big muscle of a car and pulled out of the driveway. I had recently moved back from California. My father had forced me to live with my uncle Sam in Valencia. He was tired of threatening me and using physical force to try to keep me straight, so it was my dad's last-ditch effort to save me from the bad choices I was making. He thought my uncle, with his tough love, could set me straight and steer me away from living a life on the street. That's how many of the Albanian families dealt with a wayward kid.

My uncle was a mixture of Elvis Presley, James Dean, and Dean Martin. He was always womanizing, drinking, and gambling. Yet in the same breath, he was also very strict when it came to family. He had double standards and was aggressive in his efforts to put me in line, but just like everyone else, he failed, too. The thing was, trouble followed me everywhere I went; it could've been the other way around, or perhaps it was a combination of the two. Either way, it wasn't long before I had found myself standing in front of a judge in the California court system.

I had a college buddy who was living in Valencia, and one night, I came upon him getting jumped by two men. I stepped in to help him out. I cracked them over the head with a glass bottle and wound up stabbing one of them in the side. Apparently, they were off-duty cops, and that would not fare well for me, not that I would have cared who they were. I always went the distance for my friends. When the off-duty cops jumped my friend, I just couldn't stand by and let that happen.

Instead of serving time, the judge decided to kick me out of the state. I was banned from being able to enter the state for five consecutive years. The attorney I hired would be able to get the charges expunged from my record because it was a first-offense program.

John was now back home and on the devilish and treacherous streets of New York. It appeared that no matter what avenues he tried in life, or was forced to try by his father, the roads always led back home as if he was always destined to be there. Queens, New York, was Alite's comfort zone. He wanted to somehow, someway, make his mark.

Cruising down the street, I glanced at the White Castle, a fast-food hamburger joint that was open twenty-four hours a day, busy even at that time of night. Seeing the restaurant and all the young kids flooding the place brought me back to the incident I had last year. I had gotten into a nasty fight with several guys who were harassing a female friend of mine inside the restaurant. They were drunk and out of their minds. I had intervened and wound up getting stabbed in the side of my head with an icepick. After the fight broke up, all I wanted to do was make it home so I could patch up the side of my head. What I should have done was gone to the hospital, but I was too hard-headed and didn't realize I could've died.

Of course, I never made it home. The same guys who I had fought had spotted me on the road and rammed their monster truck into the side of my car, slamming me into a tree. The truck was moving so fast that the front wheels rolled on top of the roof and almost crushed me to death. The guys jumped out of the truck with baseball bats, busted out my front windshield, then proceeded to beat me to a pulp. In order to escape, I had to crawl out of that same front windshield while getting beaten half to death.

When the police sirens sounded in the distance, that's when the guys split. I had passed out from blood loss, and when the day was said and done, I had found myself recovering from emergency surgery. The fight had left me with over a hundred stitches and staples that extended from my abdomen to the top of my head. My arm was broken, my jaw was wired shut, and my insides were a complete wreck. There were tubes sticking out of both my stomach and my head in order to drain fluids. A catheter had even been placed because it was painfully obvious I wasn't going to be getting up to use the bathroom for at least the next month.

I understood I had to take immediate, extreme, and aggressive measures against anyone who messed with me. When someone pushed me, I'd push them back five times harder. If someone threatened me, they could wind up dead. If someone crossed me, they were dead. No discussion.

On an unusually warm, fall day in New York, John Alite wore a light running jacket as he went jogging in Forest Park near Woodhaven, Queens. He had plenty of room to jog among the five hundred and thirty acres the city park offered. Jogging was one of the ways John stayed in shape, along with baseball and boxing, both sports that he loved. He would often go to Forest Park and hit the quarter mile track at Victory Field and run laps. Forest Park had a nice sports-plex surrounded by trees and bike paths. Local residents used the park's fields for baseball, football, soccer, handball, and track.

Alite had done several laps when he noticed two men on the far side of the field. They were walking into the complex from the Myrtle Avenue entrance. John tells the story.

For some reason, maybe it was my street instincts, I found myself taking a second glance at them. I really wouldn't have paid much attention to them in the first place had they been dressed in workout clothes. The fact they were wearing long winter coats and it wasn't that cold out gave me pause. It was also the way they were carrying themselves, as if they were walking with purpose and were not out for a leisurely stroll. Both of them had their hands in their pockets and wore wide-brimmed dress hats. They had them tilted down over their faces as if they were trying to obscure their identity.

One man lifted his head, and it was then I had caught sight of his eyes and followed his line of vision. He was looking across the track to the opposite side of the field. I darted my eyes to the south entrance of Forest Park Drive and saw two more guys who were dressed in the same fashion as the others.

All of them were walking onto the field, and I couldn't help but ask myself, Are those fucking guys coming for me?

I stopped jogging. It was as if my body was confused by the orders my brain signals were sending until I decided if I needed to charge and fight or turn and run. I didn't have a gun on me, but I had the suspicion these four men did.

On the left side of the field was a bicycle path, and I was contemplating running toward that side to slip away down the tree-lined trail. I knew taking that route would hold its own risks. There was the possibility someone could be waiting at the end of the trail with a car.

Scanning the area for a viable escape route, I started walking away toward the back entrance where the bicycle path was. The fact that I had quit jogging and was walking away had these men picking up their stride as they headed toward me. It was then I knew for certain they were going to try and hit me.

I had to make a split-second decision as to my exit route because at this point, I couldn't trust any of the conventional paths. I took off in a full-on sprint, kicking up fallen leaves underneath my feet as I headed for the fence line. The guys realized I had caught their move, and they started running. I knew I had to scale a ten-foot chain-link fence in a matter of seconds. The problem was that on the other side of the fence, there was a fifteen-foot drop off into a ravine, but that was my best bet.

One of guys behind me opened fire on me, and then all of them followed suit.

The distinct pop of nine millimeters and .380 bullets echoed throughout the park. The shots came in rapid succession like a heavy downpour as I leaped halfway up the fence, grabbing onto the metal links.

I wasn't even thinking how close the bullets were from hitting me or if they were too far out of range. All I knew was that I was getting shot at like crazy and that I was running. Thankfully, them shooting at me was not like in the movies where everybody's a great shot. They were not trained shooters, and they were shooting from a distance as a last-ditch effort to hit me.

I scaled the fence and flipped over, preparing myself for the deep drop into the bottom of the ravine. I fell to the ground and allowed my body to roll through the decaying leaves and broken branches, and then I finally came to a halt on top of abandoned railroad tracks. I picked myself up and started running through the woods, sticking alongside the tracks.

I didn't know where those guys were at this point; I was just glad I escaped. I figured they were heading back to the street to jump in their cars. I was quite sure they were going to try to track me down, but these were my streets. I knew them all like the back of my hand, and I knew where to go. That was their mistake.

I emerged from the trees and jogged down 102nd street and headed to one of my major drug sites, Jägermeister's, a bar on Jamaica Avenue.

My mind was reeling. There were so many possibilities as to who was behind this attempted hit. Was it from the Jamaicans? There was the time I had been with Johnny Gebert, and we shot four Jamaicans. I didn't really think it was them after thinking about it. The men who were after me looked Italian.

I thought back to a baseball bat beating I gave to two brothers, but they weren't gangster material—they were just young and not very streetwise. I had an incident in Jersey where I smashed a ketchup bottle over the heads of three guys in a diner, but I doubted it was them either. That was more than an hour away.

I had carried out so many acts of violence that there was no telling who could be after me. I had done a shooting at the Swim Club recently, and that held the most probability as to who was behind this, but I couldn't be certain. I kept backtracking to different times in my mind, trying to use deductive reasoning to pinpoint who it could be.

I learned an important lesson from this experience, and it wasn't to stay away from trouble or fighting. I was raised to be a fighter, and this little setback wasn't going to stop me from achieving my goals. What I learned was that I needed to be more careful. I swore to myself I would become vigilant in having no set routines in my day-to-day activities, and I wouldn't keep schedules. I wasn't about to walk away because I had enemies. I had too many networks in place, and there was too much money to be made.

I wanted everyone to think twice before they would ever raise a gun to me. I was becoming more and more immersed within the mob world, and I understood it would take extreme, over-the-top violence to stay alive.

It was the beginning of the end in Alite's understanding that on the streets, it was every man for himself. He couldn't depend on anyone to have his back. He was alone and being hunted like an animal in a jungle. This was not the first attempt made on John's life, nor would it be the last. The difference now was that he would always be prepared.

Me with Sammy Gravano

CHAPTER 2

Albanian families are patriarchal. John's father meant the world to him. He always wanted to make his dad proud of him, but they each had their own definition of success. Mr. Alite was a tough street guy, but not a gangster. He believed in rules and fairness, but in John's world, there were no rules. The younger Alite was maneuvering through very dangerous circles full of powerful men who required a different way of living.

When my father had caught wind of me and Joe Galliano having just shot a guy in Brooklyn over our drug business, he flipped out. It was a level of violence my father never would've dreamed his own son to be capable of. He couldn't understand what was happening to me and why I was so completely out of control. He didn't know I was only getting started and the things I would do were about to get much worse. It would be like trying to stop a tornado from spinning, as I'd go on rampage after rampage doing beatings, shootings, and murders.

In the same breath, I was giving myself one last-ditch effort to get myself off the streets once and for all. I had gone to the Barnes and Noble bookstore and had purchased prior testing manuals on how to study and pass the Series 7 test in order to become a stockbroker. I felt it was my last and final opportunity of making money legally, especially since I lost the opportunity to compete as an Olympic boxer or a professional baseball player because of my epilepsy and arm surgery, which basically destroyed my dreams.

As with anything I placed my hands on, I was overly ambitious and wanted to succeed. I never did anything halfway. I had at least ten years of testing material memorized that pertained to the Series 7 test. I read those books over and over until I was reciting their content in my sleep. If I read a question, I knew the answer without really knowing the formula—that's how determined I was. My plans were to shoot straight to the top of Wall Street at break-neck speed within the stock market companies, and I knew I could do it.

I told myself that selling a few drugs until I got my feet on the ground within the stock market was not that big of a deal. I had planned on quitting. In the meantime, the money came way too easy for me because I'd been hustling since I was six and already had a decent network of sellers and buyers. I knew everyone, and slipping back into the streets and blending in among my friends was second nature to me.

I leaned back against the park bench and held my stomach in a fit of laughter. I'd been so bogged down and stressed with studying day and night, it seemed as if I hadn't laughed in forever. A small, feminine hand swatted me on my bicep for the outburst, but it was a lighthearted smack, and all in good humor. I tilted my head to the side, wearing an affectionate smile as I regarded my girl with a special fondness.

"Stop making fun of me," she protested as she tried to hide her own laugh.

God, I couldn't love Silvana any more than I did in this moment. I remembered the time when we were in high school together. I'd make any excuse I could, just so I could go to Silvana's house and study with her. We had once taken a high school senior trip together to Disney World with our class. For her to be able to have gone on that trip was a huge deal, because her family was overly strict and protective of her. Silvana was a real Italian beauty. Her jet-black hair and dark eyes made her a solid ten, while her sweetness and kind heart put her on a different level altogether.

I would sneak in through the girl's hotel window just to be able to hold her all night long. Silvana and I would sneak into the bathroom and sleep together on the bathroom floor, and it was in absolute innocence. The entire five days of the trip, we were inseparable. Our relationship was always a virtuous one. The only thing we ever did was hold hands and hug, but I knew I loved her.

I pointed over to the brand-new, white Corvette parked in the school parking lot. "So, how do you like my new car?" I asked, proudly. I was always trying to impress Silvana. I'd do anything for her. I'd tell her I was making money, because all I ever wanted was for her to be proud of me. I wanted to show her I could make it, no matter what I set my mind to. Even though the lifestyle I was living was not the best, I could always justify it and make it right in my head. I suppose I thought of my lifestyle as being financially successful.

"Just be careful," she said with a concerned frown. A solemnness fell over her face for a brief moment, and I knew what she was thinking. She would never ask where or how I made my money; she didn't want to know, but she knew I obtained it in unprincipled ways.

"You don't have to worry about me," I assured her, shrugging my shoulders.

I knew how to survive on the streets, and thought I was pretty damn good at it.

"John, I think you're not realizing that last year, you almost lost your life. You were stabbed and baseball-batted half to death. How can you even think like this?"

I knew she was right. The streets were like living out in the wild west, but I'd stayed overly vigilant and highly alert since then.

"I know what I'm doing; please don't worry." Changing the subject, I said, "Hey, how are you doing with your studying?"

She pursed her lips for a second, probably out of frustration for me steering the conversation in another direction, but it was a conversation that would go in circles if I didn't end it. Thankfully, she let the topic go. "I've got a 4.0," she said proudly.

"I'm proud of you," I told her. The only reason I was taking college courses was so I could take the exact same classes Silvana was, just so I could be close to her. The campus itself, Queens College in Flushing, New York, served as a drug haven for me as well, allowing me to make money while spending time with Silvana.

"I've got some good news of my own," I said with a smile.

"Oh?"

"I just got my stockbroker license."

She squealed at the top of her lungs; her beautiful smile and eyes lit up with the good news. She wrapped her arms around my neck and embraced me tightly. "You are outrageous, you know that, right?" I hadn't told anyone else the results yet—I wanted her to be the first one to know.

"Yeah, I know," I teased. I grabbed her hand and gave it a gentle squeeze. "I'm going to make something of myself. If it's not in baseball, then maybe it'll be in the stock market."

Alite had been a serious baseball player ever since he was around seven years old. He dreamed of becoming a professional player, as many boys at that age do, but John attacked the sport with his entire heart and soul. Just like many young boys at that age, John started out in Little League, but as with everything else in his life, he excelled and played several positions—mostly pitching, catching, and second base. His MVP status was noted by his coaches at Frankin K. Lane High School on Jamaica Avenue in Brooklyn, where he played mostly third base on the varsity team for all four years. By his Junior year, John became the team's switch-hitting captain. As a freshman at the University of Tampa, he went from Junior Varsity to Varsity. Tommy John surgery on his arm prevented his move to semi-pro ball.

"You really are amazing," she said, gleaming with happiness.

I pulled back and stared into her eyes. "I'm just determined, that's all." I had my stockbroker license in hand at age nineteen, which was almost unheard of. Now I had the opportunity to get rich in the stock market and make my money legally. I knew the market was young enough and had room for someone like me.

"That's not all the news," I said. "I just landed a job with J.P. Morgan," I told her proudly. It was a company my cousin was involved with running, so I already had an in, but back then, it was easy to get jobs with broker companies whether I had a recommendation or not.

"When do you start?" she asked excitedly.

"Monday," I smiled. I was on cloud nine, feeling like I had the world at my feet.

In a split second and with no warning, I had a flashback. There was no rhyme or reason as to when these flashbacks would hit me. I could be in the middle of a conversation, just like now with Silvana, and a piece of my past would come out of nowhere and burst into my thoughts. I was reliving a moment when I had put a knife through the throat of some guy down in Florida. The memory was clear as day. I blocked his punch, then, using the knife in my right hand, rammed it into his gut. By the time I pulled out my knife coated in blood, he screamed out in pain.

"What's wrong?" Silvana asked, noticing the immediate shift in my mood. I refocused on Silvana, her long, jet-black hair shimmering against the sunlight. I reached out and ran a few silky strands through my fingers and shrugged noncommittally. "John…" she prompted when I didn't answer.

What I loved about Silvana the most was that she was so pure and innocent, untainted by my world. She was the calm to my storms, but already, I could feel us shifting apart. I always knew this time would come; it was inevitable. The both of us had different plans laid out for our future. Silvana's parents were old-school, and they had chosen a husband for her years ago. Once she finished her four-year accounting degree, she was getting married, but it never stopped me from loving her.

I turned toward her, giving her an easy smile. "Just thinking about shit," I said with a grin, choosing to stay elusive.

The world around me kept changing at warp speed. No matter what I did, or how hard I tried, I couldn't seem to stop the situations in my life from either accelerating and spiraling out of control or falling apart. Everything good I touched in life seemed to slip through my fingers like fine grains of sand. Deep down, I knew I was a good person, and sometimes, I couldn't understand why the cards were always stacked against me when I tried to do good. I also understood I was battle-hardened from living a life on the streets from such a young age, but the streets were where I felt most comfortable.

The streets gave me money and power, accompanied by the thrill of adrenaline rushes that couldn't be experienced anywhere else. It was the kind of excitement that could only come from living life in the fast lane. I was hoping that by working in the corporate world and staying clean, it would be enough for me, but only time could tell.

CHAPTER 3

Just as quickly as John was hired by J.P. Morgan, he was fired. He never even had the opportunity to start his first day. The legal trouble Alite had in California had come back to haunt him. His bubble of being in the Wall Street world and making money legally burst before his eyes. John's case fell under a first-time offender program in the state of California, and the agreement was that if he didn't get into any more trouble, his felony would be expunged from his record. However, Alite's attorney's office dropped the ball and never filed the proper paperwork to clear his name. The felony was still on record, easily discovered by J.P. Morgan, and for sure, no other investment firm would touch him.

Yet another door Alite tried to open, one that may have led to a legitimate career and success, was abruptly slammed in his face.

Every decent career I had embarked on always ended in defeat.

John had studied hard and saw himself making big money in the investment world. With his ego smashed to pieces, John found himself frustrated, hurt, crushed, and angry all at the same time. This unsuccessful, legitimate job on Wall Street was the last straw for John Alite.

John laments on that event.

The stress and pressure had tormented me daily. I was now done with all the uphill battles and trying to do things the right way. I was going to have money, and I was going to get it any way I could. I wanted better for myself. I wanted to have what every flashy mafia man had and more, because I knew I was smarter than the vast majority of them. They didn't know the streets the way I did. Hustling and making money on the streets had always come naturally for me. It was a life I knew like the back of my hand, so I threw myself into the streets headfirst and never looked back. I knew I'd be successful there.

CHAPTER 4

John was feared by nearly everyone in the street life, largely because his quick temper, propensity to anger, and uncontrolled aggression went along with the "Albanians are crazy" mantra. He held nothing back and didn't give two shits about who he was dealing with.

There was nothing I wouldn't do or not do to become involved with an order to increase my earning potential. I didn't know what the top of my earning potential would be, but I knew I wanted to go to extremes.

It didn't take long before I had my hands in hundreds of schemes all going on at the same time. One of the many schemes I was involved in was stealing tractor-trailers.

I used to steal tractor-trailer trucks from Kennedy airport all the time. I had friends who worked at the airport and had access to the trucking manifest. This manifest was all I needed in order to grab a container of goods and drive away without a hitch.

I'd take the stolen trucks to the dead-end street where I grew up and where my parents were still living. I'd conduct business right from the back of the truck, selling off the merchandise. The entire neighborhood was in on it, and they would all buy from me. It was interesting to note how the neighborhood condoned my illegal activities. Not only did they approve, but they were involved in it. All of us in the neighborhood having known one another for decades, we had become a tight-knit family. We were all very protective of one another, and the families in the neighborhood were always covering for me, especially when the police were after me. I was happy the neighbors approved and, in their own way, were proud of me.

We never knew what we were getting until we opened the containers, but it didn't matter to us. Those tractor-trailer trucks served as an absolute gold mine.

On another occasion, John was invited to spend a few days in Florida and hang out with some friends, get some sun, relax his brain, and just party a bit. Always getting a business deal going or scheming for a future operation, John planned to meet up with ladies he knew from the neighborhood, the Stabile girls. The girls just happened to be nieces of New York Lucchese crime family member Anthony Stabile. Part of Anthony's claim to fame was that he was involved in multiple hijackings at the John F. Kennedy Airport. Anthony was a dangerous shooter who was one of the infamous Jimmy Burke guys. But for John, nothing goes easily. Not even buying a new pair of sneakers.

The day before I was to fly out, I decided I needed a new pair of tennis shoes. There was a famous place in Ozone Park where everybody would get their sneakers from. It was called Sneaker Corner. I pulled my Corvette up to the storefront and parked right on the main street. I only planned on being a couple minutes; therefore, I left the convertible top down and the car running.

The very moment I was grabbing a pair of tennis shoes from the shelf, I heard someone ask out loud, "Whose Corvette is parked out front?" Leaving the shoes behind, I headed to the front of the store. I rounded the corner of a stack of shoes to see who was asking about my car. There, stood just inside the store's doorway, two foot-patrol cops, and they weren't looking very happy.

"That's my car," I told them as I approached. "What's up?"

"You need to come outside," one of the policemen said.

I gave a shrug of my shoulders, and said, "Sure."

The three of us stepped outside and stood next to my car. One of the officers said to me, "I need to see your driver's license."

"What for?" I asked coolly.

"You're parked in front of a fire hydrant," he told me.

"So?" I asked nonchalantly, as if it was no big deal. I was only going to be a minute in the store, no harm no foul. "All right, so just give me a ticket," I told him. I had no intention of complying. With that statement, I turned around and started to walk away, and when I did, I was hit from behind with a heavy, hard thwack to my lower back. One of those assholes had just hit me with his police stick.

I spun around on my heels with a scowl. "What did you do that for?"

"I asked you for your license," he said with an arrogant sneer.

"What are you breaking my chops for? Just give me a ticket," I told him firmly.

The policeman stepped forward with an air of authority. "Get your hands against the car."

"Nah…" I drawled out the word and shook my head, "I'm not doing that," I said matter-of-factly.

"You know I can have your car towed," he informed me.

"So, go ahead, tow the car." I didn't care. I reached into the front pocket of my jeans and took out a wad of cash. I held the money out to him and said, "Here—tow the car. Then I'll send somebody to go pick it up for me."

I knew I was being a smart ass, but I really didn't have time for this. I had things to do, and I was supposed catch a flight to Florida that night.

"I told you to get your hands against the car!" he ordered.

His patience was wearing thin, but I had no plans of backing down. I remained adamant. "I don't give a fuck what you told me. I'm not doing that."

The cop stepped up in front of me as the other cop rounded behind me. "I'm not gonna tell you again," he warned.

"I'm going to tell you," I interjected, "to stop breaking my chops and give me a ticket if you want." I already knew by now that these guys were not going to go away without a fight. There was a reason why everyone called this precinct the stun-gun precinct. The 106th precinct had been all over the media recently for stun-gunning a black kid seventy or eighty times, and then when they got him to the jail, they tortured the hell out him. Soon after that, there was another incident, whereby the police arrested a black kid, and then they tortured him by sticking a baton up his ass. Needless to say, it was a degenerate precinct full of derelict cops.

The cop in front of me stood tall and squared his shoulders. "I'm locking you up for driving without a license."

"But I'm not driving the car," I argued. "You can't do that." The problem was that I didn't actually have a driver's license to give them. I had been driving on a suspended license. My license was revoked because I was always driving too fast, breaking speed limits everywhere I went, especially on my trips back and forth from Atlantic City. I found out later, even though I wasn't technically in the car, the policeman could have given me a ticket and locked me up because the car was left running.

"Oh, yes I can," he said, wearing an all-knowing smirk. A crowd of people had begun to gather around, witnessing our little spectacle.

"I'll tell you what," I started off, but got interrupted by an older lady whom I'd never seen before.

"Leave the guy alone," she said in a frail but firm voice while pointing her crooked finger at the cop. "He didn't do nothing wrong. I've been watching what you've been doing to him."

The cop completely ignored her. He tried to take me by surprise by lunging forward in order to tackle me against my car. This was a mistake on his part, because I was already prepared for him, and I knew how to fight.

I grabbed him before he could latch onto me, flipped him around, and then threw him on the ground. He landed hard, expelling a loud groan. Having had the wind knocked out of him, he laid there for a moment, trying to catch his breath. In the meantime, his partner pulled out a gun and pointed it at me.

"Get your fucking hands up on the car!" he shouted.

"I'm not putting my hands on that car," I shouted back.

He unclipped the walkie-talkie from his left shoulder and radioed in for police backup. As he holstered his gun, the policeman behind me got to his feet. Then, they both charged me at the same time.

The both of them were trying to get me down on the ground and pin me down, but it was going to take more than two men for that to happen. With a lot of grunts and groans, I wound up wrestling them both to the ground and then held them in place using my arms, legs, knees, and every other means I could.

Pinned helplessly to the asphalt, both men were screaming and cursing at me while the crowd around me was aghast. I was able to remove a baton stick from one of the cops, and I threw it out into the middle of the street in order to get it away from them.

It only took a few minutes before a swarm of cops arrived on the scene. They jumped out of their squad cars, and all at once, dove in on me. A blur of blue uniforms came swinging at me, trying to bring me down. The funny thing was, none of them were able to contain me. The main problem was that there were too many policemen trying to get to me at the same time. All of them were getting in one another's way and stumbling over each other. I was in top shape, very strong, and fast on my feet. Combine that with the fact that I knew how to fight, and they had their hands full.

People all around me were screaming and yelling at the police for the injustice of it all. Cops were busting me up with police sticks left and right. I was bleeding like a pig. Unfortunately, we didn't have cameras on the ready the way our society does now. Otherwise, bystanders would've been able to take videos of this crazy scene.

Finally, with much energy spent on everyone's part, the policemen were finally able to handcuff me and place me in the back of a squad car. During the entire ride to the police station, I had been calling them all kinds of inappropriate names. One of them in particular, I kept calling an Irish prick.

Later, as I stood before the judge at the Queens Courthouse over the debacle, the judge asked me about the racial slurs I had imparted to the policemen.

"Your Honor, my girlfriend is Irish and German, and I'm engaged to her," I told him, explaining to him in so many ways that I was not prejudiced against any race.

The judge laughed out loud and said, "I don't see anybody here being black, and I don't see anybody here being racist." He looked at the Irish policeman and asked him, "What are you talking about? The way you wrote things here on this report is all out of context. There is no racism here."

The Irish cop was trying to charge me with assault and with anything else he could find, but the judge obviously knew the reputation of this particular precinct. They were already in hot water with the media; they didn't need any more attention. The judge also knew the cops were harassing me that day.

There was so much corruption going on during this time era within our police force, and the judge knew it. The judge looked at me and told me I was being charged with disorderly conduct, and then he issued me a fine. After that, I was back out on the street, and it was business as usual.

This was John Alite's life. Trouble, in many forms, was part of his everyday routine. He was always getting locked up for something or other, and by this point, it was part of the life he had chosen.

I simply didn't care. It was no big deal to me to get cuffed and arrested. I'd get locked up for a couple hours, and then I'd be right back out on the streets again. I knew the system like the back of my hand.

Alite's violent behavior was rapidly becoming out of control—and he was just getting started. Violence forces most people to behave with flight, fear, and respect. John's earning potential in the world would prove to be endless. Doing everything to the extreme, John was fighting and shooting virtually every single day. Violence and the threat of violence were the tools of his trade. If someone had the balls to push him, that unfortunate guy would get pushed back...but five times harder. John took a step back from nobody. Clearly and with certainty, he was letting the world know, "I'm that guy now." That guy who was in control of everything on the streets. That guy who was taking over one neighborhood after another. That guy you didn't want to cross.

CHAPTER 5

When someone comes for a known killer like John, they're not coming to just punch him in the nose, call his mother a bad name, and then walk away. They know if they don't eliminate him, they would be giving him the opportunity to come back at a later date to seek vengeance. John wasn't going to let anyone get the best of him—ever.

John's father never understood this mentality, this level of cold-blooded killing. Mr. Alite, like most men of his era, could only understand that when one had to fight, they fought their opponent fairly by using their hands. When the fight was over, they were done, and there was no retribution. Sometimes, the adversaries even shook hands. John never had the luxury of being able to choose how his fights ended. And no one would shake hands…ever.

Those I robbed could be anyone from the cartel, gangsters, or other gang affiliations. I didn't care who they were. I'd tell them straight up that I was robbing them and that I had no plans of hurting, stabbing, shooting, or killing them, but if they felt the need to come back after me and I caught wind of it on the street, I was going to come kill them next. Unlike most, I never wore a mask when I was robbing others. I had no fear of being recognized. I actually wanted my face to be acknowledged, because I wanted people to know who it was they should fear.

This exemplified John's huge ego, and in his own way, he was building his name—his brand, if you will.

I meant every word I said. I was true to my word, and they knew I'd follow through—they feared me. I could tell what they were thinking when I gave them their warning. They were saying to themselves, This guy doesn't give a fuck, but he's not planning on killing me at the moment. So I have the opportunity to seek retribution at a later time if I want to, but… They didn't have the guts to come after me. It was a mind game I played with them.

I was bold, living by my own set of rules, not influenced by anyone else's. My rules were not to hurt or kill those I was robbing. If I was ordered to kill or told to go rob a house for a hundred grand and then kill people who lived there, I wouldn't do it. It was my own code of conduct, and I expected the guys who worked under me to abide by my principles as well. I would straight up tell them, 'If you ever kill anybody in a house with me, or shoot anyone, I'm gonna shoot you.' I never robbed regular people, civilians. It was usually just drug dealers and other criminals.

I was known to be extremely brutal, and those in the mafia kept taking note of it. Because my reputation was on the rise, and since I had known Junior Gotti for a few years, I was brought into the Gotti fold. I began working for Senior and Junior both on a regular basis.

Junior would always try to belittle me in the beginning of our relationship by calling me a college boy every chance he got. However, I was the one to have the last laugh. I was positioned right where I wanted to be. I now had a foot in a very big door, and I was going to do everything I could to use them in order to gain more power of my own.

I had to think Junior had some deep-seated jealousy and insecurities because of the fact that I was educated in every aspect, and he wasn't. He felt inferior; he had to. He wasn't street smart by any means, and he didn't grow up tough like me. He was born with a silver spoon in his mouth and never matured.

I'd always think to myself when he tried to put me down, You dumb bastard. This is why I am smarter than you. I don't have to act like you.

SEPTEMBER 30, 1962
JOHNNY ALITE
QUEENS, NEW YORK, NY

I was standing before John Gotti, Senior in his office. Behind the red exterior door, there was an old wooden desk, a barber chair in the back, and a sun-tanning lamp for Gotti to stay dark for his press and public, along with a few scattered chairs and tables. He had called me, wanting me to meet him in his office in order to speak with me. As he was sitting there in his suit and tie, I couldn't help but notice the man standing off to the side. I knew who it was immediately. It was Sammy Gravano, and this was the first time I ever saw him up close and personal. As I stood there, I silently studied Sammy. As I approached Gotti's desk, he stepped forward, shook my hand and asked how I was.

"Let's take a walk," Gotti Senior said to me. When we were outside and a few blocks away, he stopped the small chat and got right down to business. "How did things go with Gene Foster?"

"I already took care of that. He's not going to cause an issue anymore for your family," I assured him.

"I have someone who needs to be roughed up. I want you to do it. Take a guy with you, and go to this club off Union Turnpike." He stopped walking for a moment and looked at me saying, "You familiar with it?"

"I'm not sure. What's it called?"

"It's the Swim Club," he told me. Senior didn't know who owned this particular bar, but I did. The club was owned by Fritzy, a captain in the Genovese family with whom I was friendly.

"I know where the club is," I told him.

"Go there. Go see this fucking bouncer that beat up Angelo's son, Johnny."

He was taking about Johnny Ruggiero, who got in a scuffle with a bouncer. "Make sure he never lifts his hands against one of our guys again," Senior said.

I didn't bring anybody with me to the Swim Club. When I parked the car and got out, someone must've seen me, because they closed the glass entryway door and locked it before I could get to it. Everyone there knew why I was there, and the bouncer I was after wouldn't come out.

"Open that fucking door, or I'll shoot you right through the glass," I told the bouncer. He wouldn't open the door, and I didn't hesitate. I shot through the glass, opened the door, and walked in like I did this sort of thing every day. The bouncer ran out the back door, and I took off after him, chasing him down in the parking lot. I shot him twice and then left in my car to take care of another problem I had.

Johnny Carneglia had asked me to take care of a problem for him. There was a beach party at the Hamptons, and the bouncer there had beaten up Johnny's son.

This time, I took Johnny Ruggiero with me to drive the car. When we got to the joint, there were about thirty guys there, all monsters. I talked to one of the bouncers, who pointed the guy out to me. Johnny and I waited about two hours for the guy and his friend to leave. We followed behind. When we were able to pull up beside his car, we cut him off a little, which got his attention. I flashed my detective badge. I stepped out of the car and walked to his driver's side window as if I were a police officer getting ready to hand out a ticket. When he rolled down his window, I raised my gun without hesitation and shot him. I put a couple of bullets in each guy, then drove off. I didn't shoot to kill them. I shot them in their shoulders and legs—just enough to send a firm message.

One thing was made crystal clear. Nobody cared if the bouncers were right or wrong or if they knew they were dealing with mafia or not; they were fucked if they put their hands on anyone for any reason. The made men of the mafia would reprimand their own kids afterwards.

The message was 'If you touch one of ours, whether you knew it or not, Johnny Alite is coming to hurt you.'

John tells another story with instant recall and clarity.

That very same week, my brother had a problem up in Forest Park off Jamaica Avenue. At the time, he was moving drugs for Larry Lutz, who was running a major marijuana business out of the city-owned park. Johnny Gebert had been running that business for years. Larry was Johnny's brother-in-law, and although they didn't get along very well, Larry ran the business for him while Johnny was in jail. My brother had been helping Larry Lutz take over that drug business when Gebert was still on good terms with me. They were making a ton of money, and we supplied Gebert some of the drugs that were going into that park before he went to jail.

My brother was handling the money and made sure everything was running smoothly in the park. Sometimes that was a dangerous job. Being out late hours of the night, it was easy for someone to hide in the bushes and jump someone. Two guys wearing ski masks had approached my brother with guns in the park just the night before. Then they robbed him of the money.

My brother and I hit the neighborhood the next day to find out who the two guys were. We got word back within two hours. The police had nothing on the number of connections and communications I had when I wanted intel. It was a kid from Brooklyn, and we knew somebody who knew them. We used him to knock on their front door while my brother and I stood off to the side. When the guy came down the stairs, he looked out the front door window at the same time that he opened the door and caught sight of me. I had a pistol, and Jimmy had a baseball bat in one hand and an axe in the other. He tried to slam the door shut, but I slipped my foot in the opening, stopping him. Knowing we could get him now, he bolted for the stairs, then twisted around with gun in hand and fired off a few shots. Flying bullets didn't deter either one of us. I started firing up the stairs and wound up shooting the kid in the back. I don't know if he lived or died. I left him where I found him and never thought about the outcome. Then my brother and me got in the car and went looking for the second guy. We never did find him.

It was around the year 2000, and I had just gotten out of jail. My brother was driving as I sat in the passenger seat when we caught sight of a man glaring at my brother through his car window. The second he passed us, he immediately made a crazy U-turn in the middle of the street. We weren't sure if we had an earlier confrontation with the guy, or if he just happened to be a little wild. I looked back using the side-view mirror, and I saw him coming up fast from behind. "He's after us," I told my brother. "Pull over. He's following us."

We pulled the car over, and the guy following us stopped his car on an angle in front of us. All of us stepped out of our vehicles at the same time. He was a big, strong guy, and he was angry. He rounded the front of his car with a steel pipe in his hand. That pipe didn't scare anybody; even though we didn't have any weapons with us, we were ready to fight. We immediately attacked him. We ripped the pipe out of his hands, then beat him half to death with it. My brother was a tough guy like me; he would fight anyone. He was very skilled with his hands—a credit to my father, who raised us to be tough. The difference between me and Jimmy was that he didn't want to kill. It wasn't in him.

Me, however, I want to kill—and I wanted to kill that man. My brother stepped in, yelling, "That's enough! You're going to kill him!" That's what I wanted to do, so I didn't stop. He was relentlessly yelling at me to stop. As I stood over the guy's battered body, I stopped swinging the bloody pipe and asked my brother, "How do you know what would've happened if we weren't together? And how do you know if he had the opportunity that he wouldn't finish you off … kill you?" As far as I was concerned, I was going to bash his head in as much as I could, and then we'd take off. I had no idea what his condition was when we left, but I stole his car, leaving him lying lifeless in the street.

CHAPTER 6

THE GROWING OF AN EMPIRE

The days of John Alite being a boxer or a street fist-fighter were officially over. He was now living in the land of an anything goes, a cesspool of murder and mayhem. John was on the front lines of a war he loved.

His message to everyone preceded his presence…that this was his neighborhood, and these were his drug spots. No one was going to make a move on anything without consequences. John was no longer shooting people to merely clip a guy in his hand or foot in order to send a message. Those days were over. John had become a ruthless killer.

It was the early eighties, and for the next twenty years of his life, it was the growing of a real empire—an empire built on unbridled violence, drugs, murders, and illegal activities of all kinds while constantly spending time in and out of jail. His life was a nonstop circus with dozens of schemes going on all at once. Alite was simultaneously taking gambling bets, hijacking goods from the airport, stealing cars for parts, selling drugs, and enforcing and performing hits for the mafia, to name just a few. The cash flow was streaming in from many different operations, and John kept track of it all in his head. No computer spreadsheets, nothing on a single piece of paper.

I was living in one of the largest upsurges in cocaine and heroin activity in New York City, and I was taking full advantage of it. The drug business was booming, and the money was rolling in. Me and my drug partner, Joe Galliano, were living life to the hilt. Neither one of us denied ourselves anything. We bought sleek and fancy cars, went on expensive vacations, and indulged ourselves with high-end jewelry and clothing.

Joe and I were all over the place, literally and figuratively. We used to go back and forth to Florida on a regular basis just to party and date women from all over. Sometimes we'd take girls with us and fly from New York to Florida for a fun night out on the town, or sometimes we'd fly girls in from Florida to party with us in New York. The beaches of Florida, hanging out at night clubs, staying at swanky hotels, meeting beautiful women, dancing all night, and drinking champagne was the scene. We knew all the clubs and their owners in both cities, and everyone who was anyone. The ostentatious lifestyle we lived was us being able to show off the fruits of our labor, and we spared no expense doing it.

One of my larger drug connections I had met early on was when I met a girl named Lorena. I met her at a bar near St. John's University. She didn't speak much English. When she told me she was Colombian, I immediately profiled her. My thoughts were that every girl who was from Colombia was involved in drug dealing, because that was the reality in the eighties.

We started dating, and sure enough, I learned that her brother was a drug dealer. Her father was a drug dealer previously and was tortured before he was killed by the cartel. He was accused of skimming, so the cartel left his body cut up in pieces and spread out in the street. They then forced Lorena's brother Henry to take over the business. They were making him repay his father's debt. I started getting my cocaine from Henry, which turned out to be one of my best connections.

I never dated any girl for very long, except my common law wife. I was always running around, and my wife had to have known that. But for the same reasons my ex-girlfriends didn't like me and got mad was the same reason they liked me.

For all the qualities they liked about me—the danger, the excitement, being popular, a moneymaker, being flashy, driving expensive cars, and giving them jewelry, they disliked me because they all knew I was running around on them, too.

In in the backs of their minds, these women were telling themselves that they could change me somehow, and that would never happen. Even in jail, they couldn't control me. That's why I always found myself in the hole. It was just my personality to not take any shit.

The one thing I never did with drugs was let myself succumb to habitual use or become addicted. Don't get me wrong, I played around a little bit with drugs, but I never let those drugs rule me. The money I was making was far more important to me than getting high. I needed to keep my mind sharp in order to keep up with all streams of income as well as staying on top of the men I was working with. Not only was I moving drugs with my partner Joe, I was also moving them with Kevin Bonner, Gotti, and Tony Kelly.

It would be a couple years later that we'd rob Tony Kelly's brother, John, who would become a government witness and testify against me in court. I'd be arrested for assault, along with gun charges because of John Kelly's eyewitness account. It would be impossible for me to fight the cases. I would have to cop a plea and run both cases concurrently and do my time in a federal prison. Otherwise, I might have ended up with a twenty-year sentence. I got a thirty-seven-month bid instead.

Networking was a big part of the puzzle, and I was skilled at the art of making alliances and keeping those relations intact, even if I didn't like someone. I knew enough to keep my mouth shut and to not speak negatively of anyone. Adverse consequences were inevitable for those who didn't know how to keep quiet. The streets were very treacherous and unforgiving that way. With everybody watching me with an eagle eye, I found myself having to constantly wear a poker face and keep my hand close to my chest.

Even though Alite lived the high life, money management came easy to him. He instinctively knew how to grow his nest egg exponentially. John fully understood that the more money he had, the more powerful he would become. Not only was he acquiring more drug partners, but he continued to obtain a large following from the street. Alite was becoming so successful that he was getting noticed by more and more members of the mafia, and it didn't take too long before he found himself partnering up with Willie Boy Johnson, who was Gotti Senior's book making partner. Willie Boy Johnson would later be known to be a cooperator as well—one who would bash the Gottis mercilessly.

Because of my mafia affiliations, ruthless reputation, and growing power, made men were beginning to answer to and run around for me. The fact that I was Albanian and not Italian was never an issue with the mob. I knew the streets more than any of them combined, and they knew it. Every time there was a problem, those same men were coming to me for the answers. Sometimes I had to take care of their problems personally. Very few were qualified for the position they held within the mafia, and any time a strong-arm was needed, they looked to me to take care of the situation.

The older men of the mafia were watching me, too. I was spending time with them on a regular basis at the Bergin Hunt and Fish Club in Queens. I was meeting up and doing business with not only guys my age, but the older men, too. The older men liked the fact that I was violent, held a crew of my own, and could make money hand over fist. Their main motives were to make money from my hard work and use me to hurt people for them. They looked at everyone as a tool, but I did what they wanted with an end game in mind. I'd use them, too, in order to gain favor and prestige among the higher-ranking members.

I realized that with time, the guys my age were no different than those older men I had been looking up to since I was a young kid. The vast majority of these made men were weak-minded individuals, and they weren't capable of pulling their own weight. This was the very reason why the majority of them needed me. They really weren't tough guys, and they certainly didn't have the fearlessness and the balls to do what I was doing on the streets. They lacked in so many ways, which worked to my advantage. I was becoming more and more aware of the power I held in my hands.

As my empire grew, I learned quickly to trust no one. Having built alliances from all over made me stronger and was paramount in helping to protect me against my enemies. I also wasn't getting into cars with just anyone anymore. I even limited my friends to a small circle so I could make sure no one was setting me up to kill me as they had tried to do in the past. Someone once had the intelligence and power behind them to coordinate four guys, possibly more, to take me out. The thing was, I had learned not to keep to a routine. Having a routine was hazardous at best. I'd seen many of my friends fall victim to their enemies when they kept a pattern to their daily schedule, and it cost some of them their lives."

With the amount of money he was making, John didn't need to go home to his house in Queens every day. He would switch it up and go to different apartments he owned throughout the city. John would either go to his house in Cherry Hill, New Jersey, or stay at a girlfriend's place. Sometimes, he would even fly down to Florida on a whim. Alite's life was like a tornado, a constant blur of perpetual movement, and nobody could predict where John would go or how long he'd stay. There was no longer a pattern to his behavior.

Because of the constant dangers lurking, I made sure to have no set routine in my day-to-day activities. Having a routine was hazardous at best. My life was getting more and more complicated, unpredictable, and treacherous. My life story had no chronological order to it. I was everywhere at once, constantly on the move, and had hundreds of things going on at the same time.

Soft lights strung high in the night reflected off the ripples of the water as rock music played in the background. John and a few of his trusted crew were at Channel 80, a popular night club that existed on the south side of Long Beach in Island Park, New York. It was a cool summer evening, and anybody who was somebody would pull up in their fancy boats and party at Channel 80.

Cigarette boats were the in-thing, and of course, Gotti had his own Fountain speed boat. It was bright red, about forty feet long, and dangerously fast. Gotti Senior would come along with Alite and his crew on many occasions, as well as Little Kevin McMahon, who would drive the boat. If they weren't docking at Channel 80, they could usually be found at either the Hamptons or Fire Island.

Kevin McMahon was Johnny Carneglia's adopted son. He would later be known as the one who lent Gotti Junior's brother, Frankie, a mini-bike. Soon after, Frankie would become involved in a fatal bike accident, one that cost him his life at such a young age. Gotti Senior, being the mafia street guy he was, recognized that things sometimes happened, and never held Kevin accountable, even though it was tragedy. Gotti Junior always did, though.

But what I loved about being at Channel 80 was having the opportunity to hang out with the New York Mets baseball team. It was one of their favorite places as well. The Mets were a crazy team to party with. They were big drinkers and used drugs, but they were a friendly group of guys. They also gambled with me, which made for a ton of money to be had. Even though Sonny Digiorgio and I were in the gambling business together, it was Willie Boy Johnson who I worked with for handling the Mets' sports bets. I was put on a half sheet, which meant I would receive fifty percent of the profits from the bets the Mets placed.

Some of the Mets players used to call me directly and use fake names when placing their bets. I would write their names down in a coded manner so I'd know who was actually betting. An example would've looked like this: 'NY Mets/Joe baseball.' Fat Mark Caputo, myself, and sometimes my father were the ones to usually call the action in to Willie Boy.

Fat Mark Caputo and I were good friends, and he'd always be hanging out with me at Channel 80. Fat Mark would later be wrongly prosecuted for the famous Silver Fox murder. It was Junior Gotti who beat up one guy and then stabbed a guy named Danny Silva. He would die from stab wounds to the chest, heart, lung, and sternum.

Junior had stupidly put all his friends at the location of that murder, which led to an open investigation. He had told everybody that Greg and Johnny Massa had killed Danny Silva, but when he was behind closed doors, he'd brag and say, "I'm the one who killed him, and everybody knows it."

That incident would be one of the first times in which Junior would begin to cooperate either directly or indirectly through law enforcement. It would be revealed later that Junior admitted to the feds that he was part of the fatal stabbing that lead to the death of Danny Silva. Even after his admittance, he wouldn't take any responsibility for it. The NYPD only had one witness against Junior, and he was later found strangled to death. After the sole witness was murdered, any other witnessing prospects recanted. Besides, Gotti Senior made a payoff, "making it go away." Junior was off the hook.

John continued the story.

A good friend of mine, Kevin Bonner, had witnessed everything. He and his girlfriend actually drove Junior home the night of the Silver Fox stabbing so he could change his blood-stained clothes. During the ride home, Junior talked freely about the homicide.

Sadly, all of us truly trusted Kevin Bonner, and he would eventually turn on all of us. He became a key witness to the Silver Fox murder in court, exposing Junior Gotti beyond a shadow of a doubt. I didn't need to scratch my head as to how Junior never got convicted from such an all-telling testimony. It was part of the deal he had cut with the government. Everything can be found in his 302 reports summarizing all the information Junior gave to the FBI.

During that time, Junior was also trying to build the Bronx House of Detention by bribing politicians. His plans were to put gangsters, made men, and other associates in his prison so he could make money off them. He would've earned big, too, because what he was building was a private institute. This, too, was in his 302 paperwork, where he admitted he was trying to open his own private prison.

In effect, with the 302s as proof, John Gotti Junior was planning on building a jail to house, along with other criminals, the very gangsters in the life that he knew.

The party scene was much of the same in Fort Lauderdale beside the ocean waters, except it wasn't. It was where Alite's eyes truly opened up to the vast number of mobsters who would congregate there on a regular basis. They'd pull up in their fancy yachts to dock at these prestigious places along the water. It was a party scene like no other, and John took full advantage of the opportunity to rub elbows with those at all levels of criminal stature. John and his drug partner Joe typically

stayed at the Ocean Manor and then would go hang out in many of the swanky clubs. His typical hangouts were Shooters, a club on the water; Josef's; or a place called Park Avenue, which some of the Genovese family frequented.

Guys like Tony were there a lot, and although Tony was from a different crew than mine, I got very friendly with him. We didn't ever discuss what we did amongst one another. We knew what each other did for a living. Everybody who was making vast amounts of money was selling drugs; it was a given.

"You want to do what?" I hissed in a conspiratorial whisper. "Are you crazy?"

"It'll be fine. I have the opportunity to skim off thirty kilos. It's no big deal." I stared at Tony in disbelief. Kilos were going for about forty thousand a piece.

"That's no chump change," I told him seriously. I didn't need to even think about it—skimming kilos was not a good idea. "Don't do it, Tony," I warned. "Just keep your head down, stay in your own lane, and mind your own business."

"Nah," he waved me off. "I've got this."

"Don't mess with these cartel guys, Tony," I pleaded, but my words fell on deaf ears.

Come to find out, that's exactly what he did. He disappeared for about two months and then came back to Florida.

When I found out he was back in town, both Joe and I had been trying to get in touch with him for a couple weeks. We were supposed to meet up and do business with him, plus we owed him some money.

It was the Colombian cartel that Tony robbed, and I knew the guys. They were just one of the many factions I was doing business with. It was mere weeks after he resurfaced that his name was found all over the news channels, and not in a good way. His head had been cut off and staked on top of a fence post. It was message to the world that no one was going to rob the Colombian drug dealers and get away with it. He had become another casualty of treachery, greed, and war in the streets, and another one of my friends who lost their life. It didn't surprise me; I knew this was all part of the risks we took living the life.

I immersed myself further and further into the matrix of the mafia and beyond. The trick was knowing how to tiptoe up to the line of danger, recognize it, and then not cross over it. Tony crossed over the line, and all I could do was warn him not to steal those kilos. I knew how to identify risks and boundaries and which ones held treacherous and unpredictable outcomes, but Joe didn't like it. My drug partner Joe became very uncomfortable with the new direction I was taking. He was no longer interested in expanding our drug business; the risks and dangers were too great for him, so he decided to respectfully bow out.

Besides the money, adrenaline rushes were one of the many things I lived for. I loved to fight. Whether it was the cartel, mafia, or anyone else, the number of guys fighting against me never bothered me. I knew I'd be smarter, tougher, crazier. The fact that I didn't feel physical pain the way most did made me feel as if I were invincible. I knew most weren't capable physically and/or mentally to take extreme risks the way I did, and that was my advantage.

CHAPTER 7

Fight at the Bar Over Drugs

There was no rhyme or reason as to when violence would erupt. It could be over the most innocuous scenarios, because even though John was smart about his surroundings, he was hot-tempered, wild, and highly unpredictable. This is one reason why his crew always called on John when things got heated in their own lives. They knew Alite would be the guy who could wreak havoc on any situation. Everyone who knew John Alite well enough called him "The Sheriff." It had become a popular nickname throughout his childhood and followed him into adulthood.

I was known to be the good/bad guy. I wasn't the one who typically started controversy, and I'd never hurt someone unless it was truly warranted. Most of the time, it was me protecting my friends or someone else.

I kept a small circle of friends I truly trusted. Guys like Frankie Burke, Joey Danka, and Greg Reiter to name a few. I had grown up with these guys since we were kids. All of us looked out for one another and had each other's backs in a world where it was unheard of.

The number of people I was moving drugs with was endless, but I had a main group of guys who I moved drugs with. Frankie Burke, Joey Danka, Dennis Pittman, Keith Pellegrino, Guy Pedon, Fat Andrew Risovuto, and Angelo Costelli. We were all in good standing with one another and enjoyed spending time together.

Everyone knew Frankie Burke because of his father Jimmy. Jimmy Burke was a suspect in the famous Lufthansa heist, whose ruthless and treacherous character had been portrayed by Robert DeNiro in the movie Goodfellas.

Joey Danka had become Vinnie Gotti's brother-in-law. Joey wasn't extremely violent, but if he had to do a shooting, he would.

Joey was a good moneymaker and a tough guy, but he wasn't an out-of-control killer like Angelo, Frankie, and me. Angelo wasn't the biggest moneymaker, but he made up for it with his ability to shoot. Together, we were one cohesive crew, and we were feared. There weren't many crews that would dare to challenge us.

"What the fuck are you doing?" I asked Frankie, groggy and half asleep. It was a ritual of ours to always touch base first thing in the morning, but this was way too early. Frankie made some joke about the sandman, then laughed. I didn't find it funny; I was still trying to wake up. "What the hell? Why are you calling me so early?"

"Daylight's burning, man. What are you doing later?"

"Nothing," I replied with a yawn.

"Let's all meet up," he suggested.

I stood up and stretched, asking, "Where do you want to meet?"

He thought for a second, then said, "Let's all meet by that bar on a 111th street and Liberty Avenue in Ozone Park."

My brows crinkled as I tried to think of the name of the bar, even though I knew the place. "What the hell is over there?"

Once in a while, the guys and I would meet up at that bar and shoot pool. "Everybody can meet over there, and then we'll go get a drink, get lunch, whatever."

"All right," I said, and after exchanging a few more words, we hung up. I had quite a few errands to get out of the way before I could hang out with the guys.

I was almost completed with my stops when my car phone rang. I was living in the era of beepers and car phones. They were invaluable tools of the trade to have with my line of work.

"Hey, Johnny." The voice on the other end was none other than Joey Danka, and he sounded a little anxious.

Curious, I asked, "What's up, Joe?"

"What are you doing?" Then he quickly added, "Are you coming here?"

I said, "Yeah, I'm on my way. It'll be few more minutes. I have a couple stops to make first."

"All right, just get here as fast as you can."

"What's the matter? What's going on?"

The noise from the bar faded, and I knew he was headed outside for privacy. "We've got a problem with some guys here."

"So, what's the problem?"

He hesitated for a brief second, exhaled, then confessed, "We're shooting pool with these three guys. It's me and Angelo, and we're playing with a gram of ball."

"Okay," I said and started laughing. "How much of that gram have you guys done already?" I knew them all too well. The both of them were big partiers, and the fact that it wasn't even noon yet didn't matter. It was the norm for them.

"Yeah, we already started."

I chuckled and shook my head at the crazy trouble we fell into on a daily basis. "Listen, just relax, and don't worry," I assured him, then added, "I thought we were all going to go eat."

"You know me," he said, "I'm a pro. I can eat on this, and Angelo is worse than me," he said laughing. "And you know, I don't have to tell you that Angelo's eyes are bugged out already." I wondered if those two would ever get a grip on their drug use.

"All right," I said. My gut told me the situation would most likely escalate, and I needed to get there sooner rather than later. "Where's Frankie? Is he there yet?"

"No. No, he's not," Joey replied.

"Okay, let me call Frankie. I'll be there in a little bit," I said, and then reemphasized, "Relax, don't do anything until I get there. Got it?"

"Yeah." There was a brief moment of silence, then he added, "You know what the fucking problem is?"

I interrupted him and said, "Joe, you're hustling those guys, so stop bullshitting me."

"Hey, they wanted to play for a gram of ball. I didn't twist their arm to play."

"What do they owe you?"

"Well, they owe us about three ounces already." I lifted a brow in surprise. Three ounces added up to about $7,500. I had no doubt those guys were pissed off and would balk about paying up. They knew they got hustled.

"Just ease off the game and don't do anything until I get there."

I hung up the phone, then dialed Frankie. "Where are you?"

"I'm on my way," Frankie said, and by the tone of my voice, he knew something was wrong. "What's going on?"

I told him Joey and Angelo were having a problem with three guys at the pool table. When I finished telling him the story, he burst out in laughter the same way I did. Neither one of us were taking the situation seriously, because this was an everyday occurrence for us. It's not as if the predicament they were in was a major one. It was more of an annoyance at this point. We both figured we'd take care of it when we got there.

By the time I got to the bar and walked back to the pool tables, I could tell the tensions were escalating. It was noon, and everyone was fully drunk and high as a kite. The guys were cursing back and forth, using words like "junkie cunts" as I stepped in close to Joey. With me here, it was now three on three, and I was the sober one.

A voice full of animosity sliced through the air. "What is he? Your personal savior?"

I stepped up to the punk who was vibrating with hostility and challenged him, daring him to start something. "What you say to me?" He stood quietly before me. I glanced over my shoulder and asked Joey, "How much do these guys owe?"

"About three ounces," Joey said, confirming what I already knew.

"All right," I said, scanning over the three guys, sizing them up. "I'll take the next shot."

One of the guys shouted from the other side of the pool table, "No, he ain't taking the next shot. We're in the middle of a game, and it's two on two."

"What the fuck's the difference?" I asked. "You guys aren't winning anyway."

Angelo held out his pool stick for me to take. I grabbed it and then positioned myself over the table, getting ready to take a shot. Once I was in position, I was pushed from behind. The very second I felt hands on me, my body immediately reacted by twisting around. Before anyone could blink an eye, I had already cracked my stick over his head. I wrestled the guy to the floor, both of us trying to get in punches on the way down.

Joey delivered an uppercut to one of the other guys while Angelo pulled out his .38 revolver. Angelo was a decent shooter, but I was on top of my guy, and he was aiming his gun at us. Angelo started shooting all around me. My eyes went wide with surprise, and at the same time, I was infuriated. "Stop fucking shooting!" I yelled at the top of my lungs. Angelo was very high and too drunk to be wielding a gun, let alone shoot with any accuracy.

"I know what I'm doin'," he barked back in his special accent, one that when he spoke, it sounded as if he were not very educated.

More gunfire erupted around me, and I had no clue how Angelo hadn't shot me yet. The guy underneath me was yelling, screaming, and fighting for his life, while I was yelling and screaming at Angelo to stop. It was absolute chaos.

As Joey kept pummeling one of the guys, the third guy got spooked and started to make a run for it. Joey grabbed a chair and slammed it into his backside while Angelo shot the kid in the ass and the leg. At least I think that was where he got shot. The entire scene had unfolded so fast, everything was a blur.

The young kid screamed and went down on his knees. I got off the guy I had been entangled with so I could help out Joey. The rush of adrenaline was pouring out of our veins, and we wound up beating the hell out of them all. When we were satisfied with ourselves, we took off. None of us were worried about witnesses or police involvement. This was our neighborhood, and we owned it. Even if we didn't know all the bartenders, they certainly knew us, and they understood to keep their mouths shut.

I jumped in my Corvette, and Joey and Angelo in theirs. At the time, all of us were driving Corvettes. My car phone rang, and it was Joey. "Just follow me," he instructed, half out of breath. We wound up going to a local diner in Canarsie, located in the southeastern part of Brooklyn. It was a place I didn't frequent very often.

On the way to the diner, Frankie Burke gave me a call, and I told him the story. He was laughing at all the absurdities, just as I was. Frankie tended to be easygoing. He wasn't one to take much seriously. He was always making fun of anything he could using his great sense of humor and wit.

"All right, Sheriff," he lightheartedly teased. "I'll meet you guys at the diner."

I put the car in park and headed into the restaurant. The rest of the guys were already inside and waiting at a table.

An older woman quickly approached me with concern. I could see the look of worry in her eyes. She leaned in to whisper, "John."

"What?" I asked confused. I recognized her from times past, but couldn't remember her name.

"You've got blood all over you," she said in a low, disturbed voice. I looked down at the light cream-colored jogging suit I had on and saw nothing. "Your entire back is soaked with blood. Everything's full of blood," she tried to say calmly, but her voice shook.

I raised my arms and twisted my upper torso while pulling the backside of my shirt to the side to have a look for myself. She was right. There was blood all over me.

"How the fuck am I full of blood?" I asked aloud to no one. I was on top of the guy I had been wrestling, so it was perplexing as to how blood could be all over my backside and down my pants. I walked straight into the bathroom and undressed quickly. The guys came rushing into the bathroom as I began looking all over my body for a bullet hole or a knife wound.

"Did you get hit?" Joey asked in an unsettled voice.

I was dumbfounded. "I didn't get hit," I told them as I continued to examine myself. "At least I don't think I got hit. I don't feel anything, and I don't see myself bleeding out anywhere." None of us could figure out how I wound up with so much blood all over me. It was as if I was the one who got shot multiple times.

Angelo stepped out of the bathroom and tracked down the older waitress. He had her find me some fresh clothes I could change into. I lucked out when one of the bus boys gave me a pair of jeans and a t-shirt. Once I got dressed, it was as if nothing ever happened. We all sat down and ordered lunch.

I was in the middle of giving Angelo the riot act when Frankie slipped into the booth beside me.

"How the fuck did you not kill me! Are you crazy?" I was still heated over Angelo trying to shoot his gun as if he were Billy the Kid.

"I knew what I was doin'," he argued back in that derelict voice of his.

"I was on top of the guy, and we were tangled up together! How the hell did you know who was who? It wasn't like you aimed for his leg. You shot him in the stomach and in the side," I contended. "That was too close for comfort." It certainly didn't appear that Angelo had a true aim, but I guess he did.

Before Angelo could respond, Frankie jumped into the conversation. "Hey," he said to Angelo wearing a sly grin, "if you wanted to shoot Johnny, why didn't you just shoot him? We all know you want to shoot him."

"What the hell?" Angelo said, obviously taken aback.

"We all know you've been trying to shoot him," Frankie said, fully intending to rub Angelo, but Angelo wasn't liking it one bit.

"Stop saying that to him. He's going to think it, and then he's going to want to kill me!" Angelo said defensively. Angelo was a good guy. He had invited me to his wedding, asking me to be an usher. He remained close friends with me, even though he was friends with and knew I was having problems with Carmine Agnello, Gotti Senior's son-in-law.

We were all eating, talking, and laughing, the conversation centering around jokes and how I wound up with blood all over me. Nobody was phased in the least over what happened. We weren't even talking about it. We didn't even know if any of those kids were dead;, nobody cared."

This was their camaraderie—it was what they all lived—what they all had become. They were all young men who were intertwined with one another in some way, each of them having reached the point of no return, full of reckless violence, and having absolutely no regard for human life. Every one of them was conditioned, numb to violence, and blinded by abject greed and power.

Everyone around John Alite used drugs a lot, sold a lot, and they all used each other to make money, everyone clamoring to reach the top of some nonexistent pinnacle of success. In actuality, it was a bottomless pit of greed, evoking an insatiable thirst in each one of them. It was a thirst that could never be quenched, and it would cost each one of them something personal. For some, it would cost them their lives, like Angelo Costelli, who was pistol whipping someone on Jamaica Ave. and 87th street, but then dropped the gun. He was then murdered— shot six times. Others would suffer a lifetime of pain and heartache.

John was under the delusion that living that life wasn't going to cost him.

CHAPTER 8

Heroin at Rikers Island

Sonny DiGiorgio turned around and said to me under his breath, "I need you to move this." I raised a brow in questioning as he handed me a thick package wrapped in brown paper. I stared at it for a moment, thinking it to be an eighth of a key of something, but I wasn't sure. I looked up from the package to Sonny and asked, "What is this?"

"Heroin," Sonny said in a low voice.

"Look, Sonny, I don't know where to move this," I told him in all honesty.

"Well, you won't believe who gave me this to give to you." I could tell he was dying to tell me who it was that had entrusted me with this amount of heroin, but I didn't want to know. Sometimes knowing was dangerous. Sonny was the uncle to John Gotti Senior's wife, Vicki. We had known each other for a while now and were in the gambling business together. We had been quite successful, but I wasn't expecting this turn of events.

As he started to give me hints, I interrupted him, telling him again, "I don't want to know." I could only guess as to who it was, but I wasn't interested.

"You have a talent for the way you move drugs," he said, and apparently, he couldn't handle the suspense any longer, so he blurted out, "Angelo said don't screw this up. The Chief knows what you're doing." We referred to Gotti Senior as "The Chief", and Angelo Ruggiero was Senior's right-hand man. I knew this would be a big step upward for me if I could find a channel to move this heroin.

"Can you get an outlet for it?" he asked, hopeful.

I pondered the question for a moment and then told him, "Yeah, I think I can find an outlet for it." I really had no idea how I was going to move these drugs. I was used to selling cocaine, not heroin. This drug was going to require an entirely different market than the one I was currently working in. "Let me think about it."

After brainstorming for a day or so, an idea finally came to mind. I knew most jails held about 2,000 inmates. Rikers Island held twenty-five to thirty thousand inmates at any given time, then add workers and employees to the mix, and we were talking close to fifty thousand people in total. Rikers Island was just about to become one of the largest banks on the East Coast for the mafia. It was a brilliant move, really, and I already had the contact person in mind.

Pete Crisci was a well-established guard at Rikers Island. I had done a murder with his brother Tommy a while back. One didn't bring just anybody in on a murder; you brought in guys you grew up with, guys you had a history with, guys you could trust. I trusted the both of them implicitly. With Pete's status of being a sergeant, he had access to people and places in the jail most didn't. Pete's other brother Joey would soon become an NYPD cop, and he, too, would prove to be a valuable asset to me.

The guys from our neighborhood who committed crimes were sent to Rikers Island to serve their time. The fact that I served time there, too, was to my benefit. Almost everyone in the jail system either knew me or knew of me; therefore, they trusted me. The product I was given to sell moved slowly at first because the inmates were hesitant to buy. I didn't understand what the problem was. After investigating why, I found out that the product wasn't that good because Sonny DiGiorgio was cutting the drug he was receiving from Angelo Ruggiero.

This was a big issue, to say the least. The drugs had my name and reputation on them, and it was my goal to sell quality heroin. I knew that by selling inmates quality, I'd have repeat customers. I wound up meeting with Angelo and told him about my concerns. He wasn't happy to hear what was going on. He then turned around and jumped on Sonny's back, demanding the product be in a better form and to stop cutting it.

Once the problem was rectified, I told Pete Crisci to spread the word to everyone that these drugs were mine and that the heroin could be trusted. Pete then started bringing other guards in on the deal in order to help distribute the drugs within the prison system. Soon afterward, a smooth rhythm of buying and selling took place between the guards and inmates.

Since the prison was located near LaGuardia airport, Pete and I chose a nearby diner to serve as our regular meeting spot. I never stepped foot on Rikers Island to do my business; I didn't need to. I only had to exchange drugs with Pete Crisci. Once a week, I'd give Pete about an eighth of a key, and in exchange, I'd get cold, hard cash. The money was usually given to me in a duffel bag or a brown paper bag with rubber bands wrapped around the cash. In a typical week, we'd pull in anywhere from twenty to forty thousand dollars. It just depended on how the week went.

Our business at Rikers Island soon took off exponentially. The channel of monies brought in from sales went from Charlie and Tommy Crisci, into my hands, and I handed off to Angelo Ruggiero, who in turn gave the money to Gotti Senior. By the early nineties, this very drug ring I established and ran would earn the Gambino family almost a million dollars a month and sometimes more. This type of generated income allowed me to not only move in and among higher circles, but I became privy to so much.

The fact that I grew up and was friends with many sons whose fathers held high positions within the mafia worked to my advantage as well. I was able to establish a deeper friendship with Mark Reiter, the father of Greg and Michael, who were my best friends since childhood.

Sadly, the Reiter family would soon fall to tragedy. Mark would wind up getting a life sentence. He could have never spent a day in jail if he had given up Gotti Senior, but he kept his mouth shut. Meanwhile, Gotti Senior was contemplating having Mark killed. What happened after that was any parent's worst nightmare. Their son Greg was killed, and his body was never found. It was presumed his body was dismembered. Greg and I were so close, I had taken the blame for a gun charge that was actually his because he had another case going on at the time. The corrupt attorney I had was able to work the system, allowing me to just get probation. I spent years trying to find out who killed Greg so I could kill them.

Mark was deep into the heroin trade as well. He was partners with Angelo Ruggiero's brother, Sal. Both men were flying in hundreds of kilos at a time. They distributed to not only our faction, but to others as well, such as Nikki Barnes and Bumpy Johnson. Those men were famous organized crime bosses who controlled the majority of the heroin trade in the Harlem area.

One of my other drug connections was Guido Russo. He was my father's good friend who lived on the corner from us. He was an Italian butcher who couldn't speak very good English. We used to call him a grease ball. Guido had a lot of connections with Europe with being able to get us cocaine.

My uncle Maxi, who was married to a Detroit mobster's daughter, was yet another connection who would bring it to me.

The Kelly brothers, John and Tony Kelly, were friends of mine who Gotti originally hooked me up with, but they were limited in the amounts they would bring. It was important to keep several sources going at once and the money rolling in."

Alite's accomplishments of being able to establish such a successful drug operation had garnered the recognition and respect from John Gotti Senior and his counterparts. John was now required to join John Gotti Senior every Saturday afternoon at the Gambino family head-quarters, the Bergin Hunt and Fish Club on 101 Avenue in Ozone Park, Queens. Anyone of any rank who worked under Gotti Senior was required to show up and pay their respects. It wasn't tolerated if one couldn't attend; there'd be no excuses accepted whatsoever. Alite explains the protocol.

The reason why Senior made these meetings mandatory was to keep the camaraderie going among the men. It reminded me of my baseball team in college. Our coach wouldn't let us join any fraternities or any social clubs. His thought process was, if we were always together, we would be loyal to one another. This was Senior's reasoning as well. He wanted everybody together to foster closeness among his men. Meanwhile, it was that very same closeness that got one killed.

We all sat down and ate together. I had a regular assigned seat at the main table which was reserved for about 20 made members of John's crew and myself. No one was ever allowed to talk serious business at the club. We'd mainly spend our time with small talk and joking around. The conversations never really amounted to much. On the weekends, made men would come from all over New York and New Jersey to pay homage to Senior, and we'd all sit down and eat together.

Even guys who would be made later on in life would only be allowed to sit at the smaller tables, not at Senior's table. But there I was, right up there with the boss. It was his way of showing I was respected as being a made man; his way of showing me respect for all my accomplishments. This gesture really brought to life for me as to where I stood in Senior's mind. It was a trust thing we had built because he and others had been watching me handle their money, not only with the Mets and gambling, but with their heroin. The fact that I had access to Rikers Island on the level I did was something that had not been accomplished by anyone before me.

Senior was recognizing my abilities to make enormous amounts of money as well as being trustworthy. He knew I was highly diversified with my social skills, being able to mingle with people from all walks of life. I was meshing with Spanish and black communities and beyond. It was more than apparent to him that I was an important asset who held hundreds of powerful connections, but in the same breath, I knew I was being groomed. It was like graduating from kindergarten and moving on to the next grade level ahead of me. Each layer of education, of course, having more responsibilities than the last. Even though I was learning all the ins and outs of the life, I knew I was a little step ahead of them all. I found a way to make crazy money inside a jail when no one else could. I was on my way to becoming a major player.

Gotti Senior looked at me as an enforcer, but different than some of the other guys. If someone tried to kill me, he took that more personal; I was always with his personal family.

Junior's ego and insecurities erupted like a volcano, and he started throwing an absolute fit. "You know what the protocol is," Junior said, full of vexation, but Junior had no say in the matter. He wasn't a captain at the time, and even if he was, I wasn't so sure that rank would've been enough to have me removed from the table.

"Shut the fuck up," Johnny Carneglia snapped. His voice boomed across the room, full of authority. Johnny walked over to Junior and went nose to nose with him, barking in his face, "You want to talk about protocol? You mind your own damn business, and you go over there," he pointed to a corner table in the room. "Take your seat and shut the fuck up."

There wasn't much Junior could do except narrow his eyes in hostility and comply to taking his seat at the designated table.

Slowly, conversations around me resumed to normal. Even though I was not an officially made man or even Italian, I was treated as if I were. The only one who talked down to me as if I weren't a made guy was Junior. Gotti Senior never treated me in such a manner. When Senior would introduce me to other people of importance, he'd always introduce me as a "friend" of his, as if I were a made guy, which was code to let others know I was part of the mafia's secret society. I had the respect of skippers and captains alike who were answering to me, and that drove Junior nuts.

Junior was like an eating cancer, and Angelo Ruggiero had warned me on a regular basis to steer clear of his godson. He'd always instruct me not to tell Junior what was going on in the mob world. Senior was constantly dodging his own son as well. When we'd all go out drinking or were headed to Florida, Senior was very adamant, always telling me, "Do not tell my son where we're going." It was painfully obvious that many men didn't like Junior around as well, and they'd go out of their way to avoid him.

Regardless of Junior's lame attempts to discredit me, I had found the full respect and trust given to me by Gotti Senior, Angelo Ruggiero, Johnny Carneglia, and other bosses within the other factions of the mafia families.

Very few men were capable of the level of violence and money-making to the degree I was, and I was doing it all at such a young age. I had strategically used Senior's son to gain access to the inside, and then outsmarted them all. I was right where I wanted to be. These men thought I was easily manipulated and controlled, and I let them think as such. I would soon do what I wanted to do, when I wanted to do it, without consequence, because no one would have the backbone to stop me.

Men like Angelo Ruggiero, Johnny Carneglia, and Mark Reiter were true tough guys, and I respected them. They didn't go to the social clubs and play cards all day. They didn't want to sit there and talk shit. They would tell me to do anything except hang out at the club to play cards and smoke cigars like a moron. I found myself looking up to them, dressing like them, and repeating the qualities I admired most about them.

They basically took me under their wing and showed me not only the ropes, but how to live large and enjoy it. They drove Harley Davidson motorcycles, convertible sports cars, fancy cars, and speedboats. They dressed up, went dancing and clubbing. They went to expensive restaurants, the Hamptons, and traveled out of the country.

By staying away from the club scene, I was able to sharpen my skills in all facets. I learned to sit back and observe people, then judge their character.

"Hey kid, is everything alright?" Gotti Senior leaned in and asked. It was Saturday afternoon, and I was sitting next to Senior at the Bergin Club. "Things are good, yeah?"

"Yes," I told him. "Everything is going well." Senior was making innuendos; he kept alluding to the fact that he knew what I was doing at Rikers Island, but of course wasn't ever going to openly discuss business. It was true, Angelo Ruggiero hadn't lied to me as to who gave me the drugs in the very beginning. Senior was more than involved in the heroin trade business; he was the pinnacle. He nodded his head, satisfied with my simple answer.

"So, where'd you go to school?"

"Franklin K. Lane," I told him.

"You went to Lane?" he responded with a laugh. "Yeah, I went to that school, too. I'd show up there every once in a while."

"You're not a made guy," John Junior rudely interrupted with a sneer. It was obvious he wasn't happy I was sitting beside his father at a table full of captains. Of course, Junior was terribly jealous and would always try to slight me any chance he got.

At this particular meeting, there were about ten captains from around the city sitting at Senior's table, along with Johnny Carneglia, Senior's right-hand man. Everyone stopped what they were doing to watch the spectacle Junior was about to make of himself. Johnny Carneglia leaned across the table and instructed me, "Johnny Vets, stay here." He had nicknamed me Johnny Vets, short for Corvettes, because of my love for the car.

I looked up at Johnny as he stood before me in defiance. "Everybody here's a captain," I explained to Johnny Carneglia, as if he didn't already know. I was just trying to keep the peace and not have a scene, but Johnny shook his head. It was his way of telling me he was in charge of this situation and for me to stay put.

"Stay here," he commanded.

I stayed seated and watched with great interest as to how this heated moment was to unfold. I could feel the animosity radiating from Junior. Senior looked over at me and smirked. It was obvious he didn't care; he had purposefully shunned his own son by not allowing him to sit at his table.

CHAPTER 9

The Corrupting of Policemen

I gave a nod toward Phil Barone's clunky old Dodge and said, "If you ever want to upgrade from that car, let me know." At the time, all my friends and me were driving Corvette convertibles, and I could tell he looked at our lifestyle with immense curiosity. I also knew Phil would love nothing more than to have some extra cash in his pocket. Every time I offered him the opportunity to work for me, his response would always be to laugh and brush me off. He had a pretty good idea of what the job would entail, so it was natural for him to be hesitant, but I was intent on swaying him.

"Yeah…Yeah…" he'd say dismissively.

"You already understand the inner workings of things, so it'd be an easy learn for you," I said persuasively. He worked in the Midtown South unit of the police department and was on the drug unit. He'd be a valuable asset to me.

"No, man. No, thanks."

"Look, we're all going to Atlantic City for the weekend," I said, then extended the invitation to Phil. "Why don't you come with us? We're all going."

Alite knew he was gifted with the power of persuasion, and he also knew he had a naturally charismatic personality. He was smart enough to know the traits he had and used them to his full advantage every waking hour of every day. He never stopped scheming and manipulating people for his benefit. John understood human nature and knew how to work people, and it was one of his major goals to corrupt as many cops as he could and keep them on his side. He explains how it was done.

Phil Barone was a policeman who lived one block away from me on Jamaica Avenue. He was a decorated detective who worked in the drug unit at the police station, but whose salary only afforded him to drive an old, brown, Dodge, piece-of-shit car.

I originally got to know Phil through his first cousin, Phil Lapree. I had grown up and played sports with him. Phil Lapree now owned a video store around the corner from where one of my friends, Keith Pellegrino, lived. Phil Barone knew Keith very well and would meet up with us at his cousin's video store on a regular basis, and it was there where we first really got to know each other. He was seemingly impressed with me, but of course, most people were enamored with mobsters and their lifestyle. Eventually, we wound up establishing a good friendship.

"Keith Pellegrino and Greg Reiter are going with me," I told him.

Phil pondered the invite for a moment, then shrugged his shoulders and said, "Sure, why not? I'll go."

It seemed as if the fish had been hooked.

When it came time to meet up with him for our trip, I looked over at his Dodge and thought there was no way his beat-up car was going to make the trip to Atlantic City. I joked with him about it and said, "Phil, your car isn't going to make it two blocks before breaking down. C'mon, just jump in the car with me. I'll drive."

We talked the entire two-and-a-half hours on the road. This would be the first time we would talk in depth about the probability of him working for me. We discussed money, sports, traveling, and living the high life. Phil liked to gamble on sports, so I made sports gambling the main topic of our discussion. This would allow me to make a deeper connection with him, using his vice to help tempt him.

"Gambling is no big deal," I said, making gambling sound inferior. "I've got a sports business."

"Oh yeah?" he asked, interested.

"Yeah, you should do something with the sports business." Glancing from the road to look at him, I asked, "Don't any of you or your colleagues bet on games?"

"Sure," he said nonchalantly, "everybody bets, but we only gamble among each other. You know—we just bet on a couple of games here and there."

"Well, why don't you start taking in some action with me?" I suggested. "Start off by just taking bets from your cop friends. You're already doing it." Here it was; I planted the seed, enticed him to expand his little ventures with me so he could have the opportunity to make some real money.

"I already take a little off the top," he explained. "I've only got about five or six cops I take bets from."

"Phil," I said with emphasis to get his full attention, "just imagine you having ten times the clientele. Think about the kind of money you'd pull in with that. It's easy money," I stressed to him, then repeated, "easy money." As we reached Atlantic City, I looked over at Phil and scanned over his attire, then suggested, "Hey, how about I buy you some real clothes?" He was wearing suspenders and was dressed like a complete slob, just like a NYPD cop on a shit salary. He laughed out loud, thinking I was joking, but I wasn't.

I wound up taking him to a clothing store and bought him a five-hundred-dollar blazer, a nice shirt, pants, shoes, and whatever else I could buy in order to dress him up. When I handed him the clothes, I said with a grin, "Here…this is so you can now look decent."

At first, he didn't want to take the clothes. He thought I was nuts, but I insisted.

"What's the big deal?" My brows furrowed as if I didn't understand. "They're only clothes." I pushed the bag into his hands. "Take them."

This was a tactic I often used, which was doing favors for others or giving them gifts in order to make them feel obligated to me.

Phil finally accepted the clothes, and at that point, I knew I sealed the deal. Phil was getting ready to go down a path he'd never return from, especially once he got a taste of the money. I knew I could now maneuver him into going totally corrupt and working under me. The fact that I grew up with his cousin gave us history, but I think that because of his son, he felt a higher level of obligation to me. At one time, I let Phil Junior live with me to help Phil out. Phil had recently gone through a divorce and was having a hard time controlling his son, who was about sixteen at the time. He was bad news and was always in trouble, so I let him live with me in my house in Jersey to help put him in line.

I knew how to make guys comfortable, establish friendships, and build their confidence of trust. I was so good at influencing and motivating others, it wasn't long before I started being able to have Phil enlist more of his cop friends to come work for me.

The fact that I grew up with most of these cops and their brothers put me in the most advantageous position anyone could ever have hoped to be in. Having known these guys for years on end was simply half the battle, especially since I had already gained their respect and trust from a long time ago. The thing to remember about many of these cops who grew up with me in my neighborhood is they were born with the street in their blood. Their past would always be part of them; it was merely tucked away. I just had to coax the street back out of them and make them feel safe with crossing over the line. I had a method to my madness. I would first introduce them to betting, and then once they became comfortable with the gambling, I would acquaint them with the loan-sharking business. I knew how to baby step them. I didn't just push them into the deep end.

Phil would prove to be a very valuable investment, as well as a close friend. He not only became my sports partner in betting, but he became another one of my drug partners. He followed me every-where I went, and when I moved to Cherry Hill, New Jersey, he wound up moving in across the street from me.

Alite's home in Cherry Hill was a beautiful property that he devel-oped into a spectacular estate. He was introduced to a woman who was going through a divorce and was selling the property. Alite bought the *property for $650,000. There was a lake on the right side once the property was entered. The home had a 3,000-foot, unpaved driveway that Alite had paved using John Gotti Junior's Samson Trucking Company. He added baseball cages, a pavilion for boxing, tree lined the long driveway, and built a two-bedroom condo for his grandmother and a second floor for the 3,500-square-foot house. He also built two other homes on the estate. Not surprisingly, none of the construction had any permits filed. Today, the estate is valued over ten million dollars.*

The deep levels of trust Phil and me had for each other was nearly indestructible. We became so close that he helped me set up the murder of George Grosso. After the murder, we met up with Gotti Junior. Phil had been infuriated over the fact that I had told Junior he had gone on the hit with me. On the car ride home, he grumbled, "That spoiled, soft, gangster boy will be a rat one day. How can you be so stupid to tell him?" We argued back and forth, but my hands were tied. I was still having to answer to Junior regardless of anything. Even if those orders had come from Senior, I'd have to keep Junior in the know, too.

Phil and me were a cohesive team, and literally near inseparable. He'd even bring me to several of Bo Dietl's annual Christmas parties in Manhattan. Bo was a famous, decorated detective, but I was already familiar with him because of the Gottis. Bo would attend some of Gotti's meetings, along with me and Richard Gotti.

He was a friendly enough guy. He had even introduced me to a woman several years older than me who lived around the corner from the Plaza Hotel. She was a gorgeous French beauty queen at the time, and we began to date.

Bo had married a woman named Margo. I had originally fixed up Margo with her first husband, Tommy, who was running a famous workout club called the Vertical Club in Manhattan. It was a unique time in my life, for sure, because all of us were all so intricately intertwined in some way. Even Mark Reiter had been living across the street from the club in a penthouse.

I was living in and among the center of Who's Who in New York. Phil and I were rubbing elbows with Bruce Cutler, Gotti's lawyer; Bo; and other famous names. With Phil knowing so many people, he was able to recruit Jimmy Iannello, who was the personal driver for Manhattan's district attorney, Robert Morgenthau. I was first introduced to Jimmy at his house in Ozone Park, where he lived with his parents. It wasn't too long before I became friendly with him, too, and then used him to my advantage.

Jimmy came in real handy when Gene Gotti and Johnny Carneglia were facing fifty years on a drug case for distributing heroin. Apparently, their phones had been tapped, and there was significant evidence. Phil Barone asked Jimmy Iannello for any information the district attorney might have about the case and who the witnesses against them were going to be. Jimmy would overhear Morgenthau talking on his car phone about his cases, and sometimes, he'd leave important papers in the car. Those papers were about investigations and prosecutions of cases. Jimmy would read these reports and then contact me or Phil if any significant news was found. It was a great setup.

Phil was always fully committed when it came to getting any type of job done. We worked in tandem doing home invasions, shootings, killings, and doling out beatings. He had assisted me with aligning the hits on Bruce Gotterup and Vito Guzzo. Phil actually had more balls than any of the gangsters I ran with. Therefore, I knew he had the balls to be my right-hand man. If guys were coming after us, he wouldn't back down. I trusted him implicitly and respected him highly.

He had been involved in a shooting once where two off-duty cops were drinking. One of them had a bad marriage breakup, and he was being belligerent in a bar. The police were called, and it was Phil and his partner who were the responding officers. A gunfire broke out, leaving Phil's partner and the other two shooters dead. Others were severely injured, but Phil walked away. He was given a gold shield badge, and later, that shield would be used by me in committing numerous crimes.

The only fault Phil had was that he was the cheapest bastard around. He would rather cut his hands off before he had to pay for something.

There is a sidebar story here. There would come a time when Alite had to go on the run and was unable to get to his major bank accounts. John reached out to Phil, asking him to send him twenty thousand dollars. John promised to return the funds when things cooled off. Phil knew John had plenty of money, but he refused to help because of his greedy and cheap personality.

I was the one who made Phil a multimillionaire. I had done everything for him. Sadly, we would have a major falling out because of this, and our relationship would come to an end. So many people in my life were always wanting my help, and I'd give it to them without hesitation, but nobody wanted to reciprocate in my time of need. That was something I would never come to understand.

Many people around Alite often wondered what it was about him that made him so charismatic, having the ability to sway and bend even the straightest of men and loosen their morals. John has been asked many times if his magnetism was based on power, money, prestige, or being known literally by thousands of people. The answer turned out to be quite simple. It was none of those.

Even though I had a serious reputation for being physically aggressive and tough, I wasn't trying to intimidate anybody. I stayed humble, compassionate, and kind and was always ready to lend a helping hand to anyone in need. I knew how to turn on the charm and come off like a regular, everyday guy who took a genuine interest in getting to know people on a personal level. The key was finding common ground. By taking a keen interest in and expanding on those commonalities we had, I was able to relate to people on a deeper level. I was able to make them feel relaxed, welcomed, and important.

I was considered a chameleon among close friends because they saw firsthand how I was able to blend myself in with groups of people. Even though I had my own style, if I was going to be among a certain group of people, I would change and mimic their fashion attire. By dressing with the right clothing, it allowed me to fit in and look as if I belonged in their world. This was just another way I was able to relate to people by dressing the part. I had done this for so long, it had become a subconscious act for me.

I was, however, more comfortable dressed as a gangster. I liked wearing mock turtleneck shirts with dress slacks and sports jackets with the square hankie in the front breast pocket. People would say I was the blackest white man around because I liked to buy all my clothes in South Jamaica, a predominantly black area.

I loved shoes, one of my favorites being snake skin and all colors. I must've had a million pairs of shoes in my closet to go with every occasion imaginable. My hair style was constantly changing as well. Sometimes I'd part it on the side or comb it back. It all depended on the look I wanted to portray that day.

I suppose all the tactics I held in my toolbox came naturally to me. I think I always had a talent to be able to inspire others to follow me. When it was all said and done, I probably had about thirty cops working for me. They were cutting drugs with me, doing robberies with me, participating in shootings with me. They even killed people with me. They were all breaking the law right alongside me, and because of this, they were obligated to me. I had them all by their shirt tails, and I was literally getting away with murder.

CHAPTER 10

Armored Car Robbery

"I can't do it, John," Robert said regretfully over the phone. I knew getting him to come on this gig was going to be difficult, but I really wanted to use a guy like him, someone with experience. Robert Ingles was about fifteen years older than me. He was a tough guy, a shooter, and he had balls.

"I already have the police car," I told him. It was my last-ditch effort to get him to change his mind, because I didn't want to use just anybody. "Having the car was the last hurdle. Everything is in place." I knew a detective who lived in the area who had an unmarked car.

"Look, I know it's short notice, but I just can't," Robert said, expressing an apologetic tone. Robert was in the middle of changing his life around. He had been in and out of drugs and was struggling to make the right choices. He'd recently become a born-again Christian and was obviously trying to follow the new convictions he held. He was a very famous gangster who beat three murder trials, and he felt he was given a second chance at life.

"I get it," I told him. I couldn't blame him for backing out. In fact, a large part of me respected him for walking the walk. Too many times, I'd seen criminals abuse the Bible, using it to their advantage in jail in order to get what they wanted. It pissed me off to see men Bible thumping. When guys would get back on the streets, they'd not hesitate to commit their next crime, and it would be done within hours of having been released.

"Good luck," he said.

"Thanks, man, take care." I hung up the phone and called Phil Barone to meet up with me at a diner.

When Phil slipped into my booth, I got right to the point and started telling him about my scheme.

"I've got a guy who works for an armored van company," I said. "He's training a new recruit because he's leaving the company, and he's all in. The new guy is going to be taking over the route by himself this week. He's fresh, has a gun, but he'll never use it."

Phil shook his head. "Man, I don't think so."

"I've been told the new guy is petrified. He's a soft kid—he'll never take his gun out, never." He remained silent, listening to my sales pitch. "Tomorrow is a holiday, and the money should be more than the normal amount they usually carry."

He rubbed the back of his neck as he thought for a moment, then looked me in the eye. "No," Phil said with finality. "I'm not going to do it, but I'll help set everything up with you."

That was fair enough—being a police officer and driving a stolen police car to commit a crime was probably too risky for Phil. "Okay. I'm doing this in four days. What can you get for me?"

"I'll get you some windbreakers, hats, and everything else you need by the end of tonight." He paused, then leaned forward in his chair with a stern face as if to drive a point home. "I'll give you my badge to use, but John, please do not lose my badge."

"You're giving me your badge?" I asked, a little surprised, because if I did get caught, he'd be in deep trouble.

"You can use it, but whatever you do," he reiterated, "please, do not lose my fucking badge."

He was overreacting. "Phil, I'm not going to lose the badge," I stated firmly.

By the time Phil gathered all the goods needed, I had secured my partner. It was Mark Reiter's son, Michael. I would work with Michael from time to time, and on occasion, he would help set up different robberies for me. He wasn't a gangster by any means, and he came across as more of a weasel type of guy, but we got along well enough.

It was Labor Day weekend and late in the day when I went to retrieve the stolen police car. I had buried it about five days before, hiding it in a local garage. I also obtained a few different license plates for switching out and was ready for the road. I didn't need to hotwire the car; I was able to rig the ignition by inserting a screwdriver in the keyhole in order to turn it over.

I met up with Michael at a diner, where we left his car for us to switch back into after the robbery. Then we'd find a place to ditch the undercover car.

The both of us were decked out in a full police uniform, courtesy of Phil. I had to say, we not only looked like bona fide professional cops, but handsome cops to boot.

I had Michael driving the undercover police car, and as he drove, I went over our plan of attack. "So, this is how it's going to go down," I started off. "This guy we're going to rob is a brand-new driver, so he's green, which gives us the upper hand. His route has him stopping at twelve stores. We have the cherry, so with that, we will pull him over after he hits his last stop." It was more than obvious to me that Michael was keyed-up and on edge. All his knuckles were blanched white from the death grip he had on the steering wheel. I thought he was going to snap the wheel in half. He was good at setting up robberies and the behind-the-scenes action. He wasn't used to taking an active role in the robbery itself.

"Mike, Mike, relax," I told him, trying to ease his nerves. "I do this every day.

You don't have to do nothing. I'm doing everything. All you have to do is drive." I had to keep giving words of reassurance during the entire drive just to keep him at a certain level of calm, which, by the way, was hanging on by a thread.

We waited patiently for the newly trained armored driver in the parking lot of his tenth store. We watched him complete his pickup and get back into his armored van; then, we followed him to his next stop. By the time we reached the Southern State Parkway, I abruptly changed the plans.

I looked over at Michael and said, "Forget the twelfth store. We don't need it. He's been in all the biggest stores already, and I'm thinking we just need to take him now." I was thinking it was best to pull him over on the interstate instead of taking the truck over in the middle of a shopping center. Besides, I knew there were only one or two cop cars that carried the interstate area. It wasn't like there would be a million cop cars on the Southern State Parkway.

The armored van started speeding, and we began to fall behind. "Mike, get on him," I said with urgency. "He's speeding, and we're going to lose him." The traffic was thick because of the holiday traffic, and because of that, I knew he must have been running late. Mike increased his acceleration, and it was then that I was hit with a brilliant idea. I glanced over at the speedometer and saw we were doing seventy in a fifty-five zone.

"You know what..." I said as a statement, not a question. "...the guy is fucking speeding, and we're in a cop car. Let's pull him over."

I placed the cherry on top of the dashboard, and it was like the seas parted for us. Cars got out of our way, allowing us to pull right in behind the armored van. The driver slowed, pulling over on the side of the road and onto a big patch of grass. Michael slipped in ten to fifteen feet in front of him, then put the car in park.

"We got this," I told Michael, who was still very tense. "This can't get any easier." I wasn't worried about anything. I was totally relaxed, cool-headed, and full of self-confidence. I had no problem doing a robbery or hurting anyone in broad daylight or plain sight; this was a cake walk.

I got out of the car and left Mike in the driver's seat with the cherry still on. I only needed two minutes to do this robbery, and the likelihood of another cop passing by in the next sixty seconds was improbable. The driver rolled down his window as I approached him. I flashed him my badge and said, "License and registration, please."

The guy looked anxious, yet responded in a disrespectful tone, "You know I'm an armored car, right?'"

"Shut up. Give me your license and registration," I barked back, "and be sure to keep your hands where I can see them." With that, he complied.

After he handed over his license and registration, he put his hands up on the steering wheel. I pulled out my handcuffs and cuffed his hands to the wheel. My actions had the driver confused and shaking like a leaf.

"I'll be right back," I told him. I walked to the driver's side of our stolen police car and planned on handing over the license and registration as if I was giving them to Michael to run a check with the station. My plan was to go back to the armored driver and tell him there was a warrant out for his arrest. Then I was going to leave him cuffed in the van, take the money, and run. It was as simple as that.

As I handed over the documents to Michael, immediately, I could tell something was wrong. I looked at his eyes, which were full of panic. He glanced back in the rearview mirror, speechless and fixated on what was behind him. I turned to witness a cop car pulling in behind the armored van, his lights flashing on full force.

"Oh, fuck," was all I could say.

Michael was about to crawl out of skin, his nerves shot. "Mike, get the fuck outta here, and go to the diner," I instructed.

"John," he began to say.

I cut him off. "Just go to the diner and meet me there," I said more firmly. Every second counted here, and I need him gone from the scene so I could try and talk my way out of this.

He was like a deer in headlights, frozen, not comprehending my words. He wasn't moving, and I had to refocus him. "Listen to me, dammit," I growled. "Get out of here now, Michael. That cop is not going to chase you, because he doesn't know what's going on. You pull out nice and easy, as if your job was done here, and go to the fucking diner. I will meet you there."

"Okay," he said, taking a deep breath and letting it out slowly. "I'll leave." I stepped back from the car and let him pull away. I walked back toward the van with a cool and confident stride, as if I had complete control of what was going on.

"What's going on?" the driver asked in a shaky voice.

I ignored him as I reached through the van's window and un-cuffed the guy. At the same time, the cop behind us had pulled out his megaphone speaker and said, "Officer, officer."

I raised my right hand and gave him a signal with my index finger as if to say, I'm busy. Hold on, I'll be with you in a moment. With that particular gesture, the cop was unsure of what to do. I don't think he expected to be brushed off like that. He just sat there a little dumb-founded, especially when Michael drove off. I know he was thinking that he was just backing us up, as police officers do for one another, to ensure everyone's safety.

Knowing I was going to have to confront the policeman, I had to lose the badge.

I couldn't have the other policeman getting a hold of Phil's identi-fication. If he did, Phil would have been in deep shit. Inconspicuously, I dropped Phil's badge on the ground.

With a side glance at the driver, I told him gruffly, "Get out of here."

I then started to walk away. The kid stuck his head out the window and boldly said, "You never gave me back my license and registra-tion."

The cop started yelling at me, demanding to know what was going on, but I ignored him as I walked back to the van, pissed off at this kid's stupidity. "Do you want to get fucking arrested?" I asked in a threatening tone that promised a beating to go along with his arrest.

"The other officer took it," I quipped "He got another call. It's going to get mailed back to you."

It was obvious this guy really didn't want to leave without his documents, and that pissed me off more. "Get lost!" I barked angrily. It was then he decided to take me seriously, shut his mouth, and drive away.

I strode over to the cop car as if I didn't have a care in the world. "What's going on?" the officer asked.

Responding with poise and confidence, I told him, "I was driving on the other side of the highway with my wife and kids, and this fucking guy came out of nowhere and cut me off. He almost hit me and my family." I was a master bullshitter, always having my wits about me and able to make up an alibi on the fly. "We fishtailed, almost causing several accidents at once, then wound up on the side of the road facing the wrong way of traffic. My wife was the one driving, and I've got to tell you, she was pretty shaken up. That cop you just saw was a detective. He had seen the whole thing unfold. He pulled over to see if we were all right." So far, it appeared as if the officer was buying my story, so I kept going. "I got in the car with the detective to chase him down." I rubbed the back of my neck as if I was still trying to cool off from the incident. "I swore he was driving under the influence, but he checked out clean."

The officer nodded his head as if he understood, yet he had puzzled look on his face. "Well, who was in the armored van?"

Since he didn't ask me what kind of car that side swiped my wife, I responded back quickly as if he should've known, "It was the armored van."

"What?" he responded in disbelief. For some reason, he started asking me all kinds of questions pertinent to the scene. I was having to duck and dodge his questions, giving him vague answers.

"Where does the other cop work?" he asked.

"I don't know," I said holding out my hands. "I'm not in his district."

He raised a brow and scanned over my police attire. His eyes moved slowly, starting from the top of my hat, then to my jacket, and down to my shoes. "Are you on the job?

I said, "Yeah, I'm on the job, but I'm on the job in Queens." From what I had been told, depending on the day of the week, the police are assigned a specific color to remember. If another policeman asked another man of uniform what that color was, they would be required to respond with the correct answer. Because of this, I purposely chose a county far away from his jurisdiction so I didn't get asked to name the color of the day.

"Well, what brings you out here? I know all the precincts, you know?"

"I'm at the 102nd." I kept waiting for the shoe to drop and for him to ask me my name, since I didn't have a badge on while I was supposedly working. "I was out here holiday shopping with my family."

He reached inside his car and pulled out his radio. He then called in to his precinct, and the entire time, I was thinking to myself, If this cop holds me, I'm fucked.

I tried to keep him distracted from his communications. I interrupted, asking, "Can you please take me to the other side of the road where I left my wife and two kids?"

He paused, looked over my shoulder and past me as if trying to look for a car parked on the other side of the road. "Where?" he asked, confused, not seeing anyone.

I pointed off in the distance behind me. "She's right on the other side of the road on the grass, some ways back. She was shaking and crying. We almost crashed into the wall."

"Alright, get in," he said as he hung up his radio.

Relieved I had convinced him, I jumped into the passenger seat with hopes of not letting this situation escalate out of hand. I needed to smoothly put an end to this catastrophe. The key was to keep diverting the cop from asking all the right questions, specifically my name. He drove down the road a little way and when we approached the next exit, I instructed him, "You can get off on this exit. This is where they were."

He took the exit and pulled off the side of the road and onto the grass. He scanned the area, asking, "Where's your wife?"

"I—well," I stammered looking out of sorts as if there should've been a wife and two kids left here. "She was right here!"

"Where?" he asked, confused.

"I don't know," I replied, sounding just as confused as the policeman. I calmly got out of the police car as if I was going to look for a car that would suddenly appear out of nowhere. He followed suit and started walking on the grass beside me. "I don't know where the fuck she went," I told him. The inflection in my voice was one of disbelief, as if my wife abandoned me.

I kept walking, heading toward the exit ramp as if to see if perhaps they had moved the car farther down the exit to get off the main parkway. At this point, we were far enough away from his car that I knew I could get the lead on him if I were to take off on foot. So that is exactly what I did.

I burst out in a full-on sprint and darted across the busy highway. It was in this moment, the cop knew he'd been duped and I was a fake. There was no question in my mind that he was going to come after me. He'd want to capture me in the worst way possible.

I thought, Oh, my God, because the exit was right there, and I knew what he was going to do when his cruiser disappeared off the exit where we had stopped. He was planning on coming back around, thinking he was going to catch me on the other side of the highway.

So I bolted back across the highway to where we were pulled over and ran as fast as I could. I ran down the very exit the policeman just took, knowing he couldn't backtrack, especially because of the heavy traffic.

I kept running, nonstop at full stride, until I came across a shopping center. I slipped inside to catch my breath as I made my way into a clothing store. I purchased a new shirt, jacket, and a hat. I changed my clothes in the bathroom, then placed all my police garb in the trash.

The next step was to get to the nearest payphone to call a taxi. I waited patiently inside the mall for the taxi to arrive. I had the driver take me to the designated diner where Michael was waiting for me.

I was at a loss for words when I saw Michael; all I could say when I met up with him was, "Muthaaa-Fuckaaa." There was at least six to eight hundred thousand dollars in cash that had slipped through my fingers. The money was right there. It was the easiest thing I've ever had the opportunity to do, and the odds of a policeman showing up was one-in-a-million.

By the time I got home, my father was irate. I found out that Phil Barone had complained to my father over the fact I had lost his badge, which put me in a very big argument with my dad. "You took Phil's badge and then threw it out?" my father would yell. He was shouting at me, not able to complete a cohesive sentence, he was so mad. It was, you this! and, you that! I was very pissed off at Phil for pulling my father into this.

I called Phil and went to meet with him. We had a falling out, the both of us yelling at each other in a fit of rage. "Are you out of your fucking mind?" I yelled at Phil. I never wanted my father to know the ins and outs of my crimes. My father was my life, and he never understood the world I lived in. He was just involved with gambling and the sports business, and nothing more. "You told my father I had your badge and we tried to rob an armored van? Are you out of your fucking mind?"

"Yeah, man, I need my badge," Phil said furiously. 'I told you, whatever you do, don't lose my badge!"

I closed in on Phil and said in a low, gravelly voice, "Don't worry. I'm going to go back and get your fucking badge tonight, you jerk off." I'd be pissed off at Phil for a while for going through my father to get to me. "I'll find it. I know where I was standing when I dropped it."

I went back to my father later that day, having to explain to him more than I wanted to. "Listen," I told my dad, "what are you, nuts? Do you really think Phil is an innocent cop? You think he's only in the sports business?"

Surprisingly, my father sat and listened intently, soaking in the information. "Do you realize he's in every other business with me? Did you know he's in the drug business with me? And the murder business?" I bombarded him with rhetorical questions. I was on a roll. "Well, let me tell you something, Dad, did Phil tell you when he gave me his badge that he was in on it? He was one of my fucking partners, and he was getting an equal percentage from what we'd get from the armored van." Even though my father wasn't happy, this at least cleared the air, and he backed off.

Everybody thought I was crazy for going back to the scene of the crime to retrieve a police badge they thought was going to be impossible to find. I went looking for it anyway that night with a flashlight. I found it with no problem and gave Phil his badge back.

Despite our disagreements and arguments, Phil and I still worked well together. We planned several shootings, murders, and drug dealings together over the years.

We both did a home invasion of Tommy Karate's drug house. Tommy Karate Pitera was a well-known soldier in the Bonanno Family. It was a brazen move, messing with Tommy the way we did, but the both of us were bold, wild, and fearless, too. Together, Phil and I took about $120,000 from Tommy's house. I could never stand the guy. He was a junkie, a heroin addict, and a fucking serial killer. Not only did he kill guys in and out of prison, he also killed young women and took pleasure in chopping up their bodies. That's not what being part of the mafia was. He wasn't a gangster; he was a fraud.

The warped and twisted mindset some of these men held were as if they were deranged psychopaths who deserved to be taken out. One by one, the streets would eat everyone up in one way or another, devouring the human mind, body, soul, and spirit. One just didn't know who was going to be the first to go, or of course, when.

All I could do as bodies were dropping out in the most horrific of ways on a daily basis was to not to slow down and think on it for too long. I was losing my friends and associations left and right, whether incidentally, accidentally, or purposefully. There were people like Joe Mathis, my best friend from childhood, who died in a car accident at a young age. Then there were the Gollotti brothers, who had gotten into a huge argument. James shot and killed his brother, Joey, with a shotgun by accident, blowing his head clean off. The fact that they had a gun out on the streets between the two of them in the first place showed their lack of mental clarity. Of course, the impromptu murders and planned hits were a story of their own. People like Scott Schumann, who was shot thirty-four times and killed—the fact that the murderer felt they needed to dispense thirty-four bullets into a body told me they had lost more than their mind.

The point was, I was surrounded by violence and tragic deaths nonstop. The only way to survive was to keep moving forward and to have a mental strength of steel. I had to accept everything in its reality, deal with it head on, then push it behind me, never allowing myself to look back ever again. Most men cracked, some went insane, others took their lives. I had to keep my mind sharp and not succumb to the mental pitfalls or let emotions get in the way. As soon as one task was done, I compartmentalized it, then focused on the next task at hand. That's what it would take to not end up like one of them.

CHAPTER 11

Bus Story of Uncontrolled Anger & Violence

Alite would be arrested over forty times throughout his life and spend time behind bars in many states. John had a police record that went on for pages, but he couldn't care less. He was currently out on bail, dealing with two cases against him, one of them being a deadly weapon assault case, for which he was looking at facing at least twenty years in prison.

John's life was all about violence twenty-four-seven, and it just wasn't for Gotti Senior. Because Gotti was part of the Gambino family crime faction, Alite had to work under their entire family structure. He also had to look after himself and his own burgeoning empire, as well as his very own crew.

Violence and aggression were the only things that were understood on the streets. He who was most feared controlled the streets. John's reputation had to be one of the most feared in order to keep himself and his crew untouchable. Right or wrong, John Alite protected all of them to the best of his abilities.

John's violent nature was like a faulty time bomb: highly unpredictable and very deadly. He was a force to be reckoned with. No one was able to control or take the edge off the Alite anger once it reached a point of no return. Sometimes it wouldn't take much in order for his temper to erupt, and woe to anyone on the receiving end…

My father took the window seat as I slipped in beside him, taking the aisle seat near the last row of the bus.

I had already taken stock of my surroundings; it was a deep-seated habit of mine to be painstakingly aware of who and what was around me at all times. I was in constant survival mode, paying attention to entrances and exits everywhere I went, while watching everyone's movements. A kid about my age wearing army fatigue pants was sitting alongside of me. I noted the young couple sitting behind me in the last row. My mind was in a million places at once, as it always was. Thankfully, I was sitting in the type of seat where one could lean their cushioned chair back and relax. It was steaming hot out, and I had a pretty bad headache. I start reclining my chair, and instantly, the back of my chair was kicked extremely hard, accompanied by a "Motherfucker."

I twisted my body around and glared at the kid as if he had three heads. It was blatantly obvious he didn't like me leaning my chair backwards, but he could've asked me to not lean back if it was both-ering him.

"Whose fucking chair are you kicking?" I demanded to know. He instantly shrunk back and avoided eye contact. I glanced at the girl he was sitting beside, and I could tell she had attitude just like he did. At minimum, I figured the guy at least got the message not to fuck with me. I turned back around in my seat, and in a threatening tone, he said something about having a knife and that he was going to pull it out on me. The other guy beside me murmured something equally threatening. I couldn't believe it. I did nothing but recline my chair in order to relax in a few moments of silence, and all of a sudden, the people around me were in attack mode.

I turned my head and told my father point blank, "Get off the bus." It was a tone that told him the incident triggered my quick temper, and I wasn't going to put up with their attitudes. I had no patience for guys who acted tough and thought they were the shit when they were really soft and weak. It irritated the hell out of me.

I didn't need to tell my dad what was about to go down; he already knew me too well. He shook his head and said in a low voice, "No, John. I'm not getting off the bus."

The guy behind me stood up and reached above his head to retrieve his bag from the baggage area. I assumed it was to get his supposed knife.

I slid my hand to the backside of my waist, where I held a gun between my jeans and belt.

"Go ahead, motherfucker," the guy beside me said, catching my move as he lifted his chin in challenge. He spoke as if he were going to jump in and help his brother. This time, however, they chose to mess with the wrong guy.

"Dad," I said very calmly, yet sternly, "At least get up in the front row, please."

My father's eyes said it all, and his voice projected such desperation. "John, please," he begged, "you've got two cases against you right now."

My eyes fluttered closed for a brief moment as I tried to contain my failing patience so I could reason with my father respectfully. "Dad," I said between clenched teeth, repeating the words slowly and concisely, "Get—off—the—bus." No matter what he had said or how convincing he could be, nothing could sway my anger once it took on a life of its own. His lips thinned, and he crossed his arms in an act of defiance, telling me he wasn't going budge an inch. I really didn't want him to witness what I've been capable of for years. I've tried to keep him from that part of my life.

"All right," I said aloud to no one in particular. The bathroom on the bus was only a few steps away. I stood to my feet with the intention of having a moment to collect myself in privacy, but it wasn't to try and calm down. I took a few minutes in the bathroom so I could switch tactics and plan my attack. I was vibrating on the inside with violence and a need for retribution that was indescribable.

Staring into the tiny mirror on the wall, I didn't even see myself as I was jolted back into a memory when I was standing before Mike Livigi in Port of Calls. Open your mouth again, and I'll shoot you, I remember threatening while pointing a .45mm at him.

He turned his head and spit on the ground like a tough guy, then looked me right in my eyes with a sneer. Fuck you, I recall him saying, while he spat.

The bullet went through his chest before my gun could fully recoil. I didn't even give him time to take his next breath. His eyes screamed out in pain as he dropped to the floor, unable to breathe. I grabbed a ceramic mug off the nearby table. I reared back and brought the mug down across his face, breaking the ceramic mug while he was laying on the floor, trying not to die from a bullet hole to the middle of his chest.

I snapped back to the present, thinking those guys sitting outside the bathroom walls were going to get the same merciless shooting. Recounting all the times I warned different guys who were just too stupid to see that they just ran into a man whose eyes should have told them that I was going to do what I said. My only concern was how to get my father out of my way. I needed to finish this job whether my dad was present or not.

My mind was made up, and the plan was simple. I would step out of the bathroom and then shoot the guy in the head with no warning. I wouldn't even look back as I'd walk up to the bus driver and tell him to stop the bus so I could get out. That was my big plan. I knew it sounded crazy, but it didn't bother me that other people were going to be a witness to a murder and see all the blood and guts that came with it. I didn't give a fuck. My only contemplation was that after I shot the guy, how was I to get out of the bus? My thoughts were, most people were going to be afraid, and they would freeze in shock.

By the time I slid the bathroom door open and stepped out into the aisle, I was fully prepared to shoot that kid. It wasn't the kid who kicked my chair I was going to shoot; it was the other one. The guy who was sitting beside me who just had to step in like a tough guy, but wasn't.

I took one more step forward, away from the bathroom, one second from pulling the trigger and ending his life. I think he knew what I was going to do, because he sat there in panic mode, staring at me, wide-eyed in fear. "Listen, man, I'm sorry," he gushed out, profusely apologizing several times over before he even took his next breath. "I'm so sorry."

It was as if a cold wave of water washed over me in that moment, his apology being enough to snap me out the tunnel vision I was living in.

I glanced at my father, and the look on his face told me he said something to warn this kid of his coming demise. Neither one of these guys knew just how lucky they were to have my father there to intervene, because I was just going to walk out of that bathroom and shoot them in the head with a bus full of people.

I didn't give a shit as to how many witnesses there were. I just wanted my father to get off the bus, get him as far away from the violence as possible. Honestly, that's all I cared about. I didn't give two cents about the lives I was about to take or how their families would feel.

I took a deep breath, then slowly exhaled the toxic anger I held against the guy and held up my left hand. "No problem," I replied to him as I released the grip I had on my pistol.

I sat back down and sunk into the seat beside my father and looked at him. "You do realize, I'm still steaming at this other kid," I told him. "Nothing's really changed in that regard."

He hung his head for a moment, then lifted his chin to stare at me with those pleading eyes of his, but it wasn't going to work. "Dad, get off the fucking bus."

"No, John," was his immediate response.

I clenched my jaw, really needing him to leave. "Go sit in the front of the bus, then," I said, compromising, while giving a nod in that direction.

Finally, my father relented and got up. He found a seat toward the front of the bus. Once my father was out of the way, it was game on for me. All I could think was how stupid this kid was. He was looking at me as if he were a tough guy and could take me on. He had no idea what I was about to do to him.

I pulled out my pager and messaged my two cousins, telling them to meet me at the bus station asap. We used special numbered codes on our pagers, and in so many words, I was able to tell them something was about to go down. After I messaged them, some of my rage had dissipated, which allowed me to think a little more levelheadedly.

Something inside of me, something I couldn't explain, gave me second thoughts of killing that kid. It wasn't like me to give mercy, but I almost always went with my gut instincts. When the bus reached its destination in Manhattan, everyone disembarked. The area was packed full of people, but not a lot of cops were present. I made my way to the front of the bus and told my father to go get in my cousin's car and wait for me there.

With the nod of his head, I was glad to see my dad finally comply. I met up with my cousins, and we took off to catch up with the kid I wanted to shoot. I caught him right on the street, and then all my fury unleashed. I pistol whipped him while my cousins stood watching and guarding. There was no interference; no one would intervene while I mercilessly beat him down right there on 42nd street, right in front of God and everybody. It was fast and quick, and justified in my mind. The guy had stepped out of line, and he disrespected me. He thought he was slick, but he was arrogant, figuring there was two of them and only one of me.

The violence I had wanted to dole out over that situation was extreme, but I was a gangster. Violence and mayhem freely flowed through my veins. I lived it, breathed it, and justified it in all of my actions. Despite my own violent nature, I never would have kicked anybody's chair. I would have never dreamed of it; it was important to me to exude a level of humility. But I knew one just doesn't become an asshole overnight, and the problem with those guys was the fact that they were getting away with wreaking havoc on innocent people. I knew it wasn't the first time those kids were acting like jerk offs, and in my mind, it was time for them to stop.

If I wasn't the guy who stepped in his path to set him straight, he would've gotten away with his shitty behavior for another five years or so. I was fairly certain that after having jumped him, he'd think twice before treating people of society with disrespect.

I suppose this was a prime example of why I was called Sheriff. I lived by my own set of rules, ones that I could live by, and if somebody told me to go rob a house for a hundred grand and kill the people inside, I wouldn't do it. I was so adamant about not killing innocent people.

CHAPTER 12

Stolen Car Gives Comic Relief

John Alite is a serious, deadly mobster, but he is not without an amazing sense of humor. Anyone who knew him then, or knows him now, can attest to the fact that John loves to laugh, have a great time with his friends, and basically loves to "break-balls."

"Hey, Johnny," Michael greeted over the phone line. "What are you doing right now?"

"Nothing, what are you up to?" I asked, not having heard from Michael in a long while.

"I'm in somebody's car," he replied, chuckling.

If I had to guess what his statement was about, it would mean he just stole someone's car. I just shook my head and laughed. "Come pick me up," I told him, knowing this could be nothing short of entertaining.

About ten minutes later, a brand-new Cadillac pulled up in front of my house. I opened the back door of the car and jumped in. "What the hell are you guys doing?" I asked, fully amused.

Michael's brother-in-law, Kevin, twisted around from the front passenger seat and said to me with a wide grin, "We just stole this car and thought we'd go for a joyride."

"What the fuck are you doing with this car?" I asked Mike.

Kevin was the car thief, but Mike didn't need this car for the money—he had money. Michael was in his mid-twenties and was a tough, good-looking, blond-haired, blue-eyed Irishman who loved to laugh. To him, this was just about having fun. He was one of my friends who would stay loyal to me. I would always trust and respect Michael.

"We're just having a little fun, Johnny," Mike said as he pulled away from the curb. "I don't know, Kevin can do whatever he wants with it."

After a few minutes of laughter and catching up on lost time with each other, the car's phone rang. Michael glanced down from the road and read aloud, "The caller I.D. says, 'Mom.'"

"What the hell," Michael said as he reached for the phone. He placed the phone on speaker so all of us could hear. "Hello," Mike said cheerfully.

"Hello, Tommy," an older woman's voice greeted.

"No. This is not Tommy," Michael responded with a grin.

Confusion lined her voice as she asked, "Who is this?"

"Oh, I'm a friend of Tom's."

"Well, can I speak with Tom?" she asked.

"No, he's not here," Michael answered.

"Well, where is Tom?"

"I really don't know," Michael retorted with a small chuckle. "I just stole his car."

"What?" the mother clipped back disbelievingly.

Michael's brother and me were holding back our laughter, clutching our guts so we could let the conversation play out.

"Say—do me a favor. Tell Tom we have his car, would you, mom?" Michael said, then immediately burst out in laughter.

"Where is Tom? You know, he never calls me anymore," the mother said disappointedly.

Michael started engaging her in a real conversation and began joking around with her. With Michael's light laughter and easy-going demeanor, I could understand how this woman could perceive this as being one big joke. Michael was so funny and charismatic, he literally had Tom's mother laughing along with him. It was all any of us could do to contain ourselves.

She was probably a very lonely woman and bored because she was finding this situation to be very entertaining. Eventually, she asked again as to where Tommy was, and Michael gave her the same answer. "I'm not kidding with you—I have his car," he said. "Hey, do me a favor and tell Tom I have his car."

"Give back my son's car," she said on a half-chuckle, still not sure if everything was a joke.

"Nah, we don't really want to," Michael responded in a relaxed manner.

For some reason, Michael's brother opened up the glove-box to find a bundle of cash. He pulled it out and counted out five thousand dollars. "Why does he have all this money in his glove-box?" he asked out loud.

There was a gasp that came out of the speaker, which could only mean one thing: she finally realized we were being serious. There was an immediate click, and we knew she had hung up the phone.

We were doubled over in laughter, unable to form a cohesive sentence, we were laughing that hard. Mere seconds went by before the car phone rang again. Michael placed the phone on speaker and said, "Hello."

"Please, give me my car back," were the first words spoken in panic. "I won't call the police, just bring it back," he pleaded.

"Does it look like we give a fuck if you call the police?" Michael said, then asked curiously, "And hey, why don't you ever call your mother?"

"What?" he asked, shocked.

"What kind of son are you? You don't ever call your mother?" Michael asked, intrigued. "The only reason why you're talking to your mother is because we stole your car."

"Oh my God, please—please, don't wreck my car," he begged, but his words fell on deaf ears. "Don't do this. Look, I'll pay you to give me my car back," he pleaded, now trying to negotiate.

"Not interested," Michael told him.

I had no idea what Michael was going to do with the car. Maybe he had a delivery for it. A lot of car places that needed parts would work with car thieves such as Michael. They'd tell Michael what cars they needed and how much money they'd give for a specific make and model. Michael was skilled at being able to scope out cars and then heist them.

"Well, how much you getting for the car?" he asked, knowing it would be sold. "I'll pay you for the car," he said in desperation.

Michael took a moment's pause as if he were considering.

"Well, I've already got five grand out of your glove box," he said, thoughtfully. "You're gonna have to do better than that if you want me to give back your car."

"I promise, whatever you want. How do we make this arrangement to get my car back?"

"How much do you want to give me for your car?" Michael asked. I couldn't believe they were negotiating, and it was more hilarious with each counter-offer price the guy came up with because Michael would say, "Nah, that's not enough. Forget it." Michael was just toying with him to see how high he'd go.

"Why do you care so much about the car?" Tom burst out, tired of getting the run-around.

"Let me ask you this," Michael started off. "Why do you have five thousand dollars in cash in your car? Are you a drug dealer or something?"

"Oh my God, I swear to you, I'm not," he said hysterically.

Michael's inquisition was nonstop as he kept asking a slew of questions, one after the other: "Do you have kids? Are you married? Why do you have this cash in your car?" Tom was quiet for a moment, probably in shock.

"Do you have a girlfriend?" Michael inquired.

"No, I don't," Tom answered back.

"Well, what kind of son are you, anyway?" Michael asked, full of ridicule. "Your mother said she hadn't talked to you in a week. I tell you what you're going to do. You're going to call the florist and send your mom flowers. Then call me back with the confirmation number so I can check you did it." He paused for dramatic effect, then said, "Or I will burn the car."

Five minutes later, Mike got the confirmation that Tom sent flowers to his mother. Tom still didn't know if he was ever going to see his car again or if we were going to make him jump through more hoops.

When the guys were finished having their fun, Mike called Tom to say it was his lucky day. Mike parallel parked in front of some random store in the city where he told Tom he could find it.

"Hey, isn't this where your after-hours club used to be, on the corner?" Mike asked as we were getting out of the Cadillac.

"Oh shit, you're right." That's where Mike and my brother-in-law went to collect my drug money. I'd also get machine money from my Joker Poker vending machines and my weekend's take from the bar. I had the club for one year before I closed it down several years ago. It all started over a nonsensical argument, one that I can't even remember. One minute everyone was happy, the next, an off-duty cop was shot and fighting for his life on the floor of my club. The club closed down after that.

I had another incident, but it was in my after-hours bar. My cousin, Patsy Adrianna, and his cousin, Nikki Pasquel, were running my after-hours bar at the time. A fight broke out at my place, and another off-duty police officer wound up getting shot in the stomach and chest. The cop agreed not to identify anyone and keep his mouth shut, but it was going to cost us.

The cop wound up staying true to his word. I wanted to on my end, but my cousin through marriage, Nikki, never made the sixty-thousand-dollar payoff. He fucked me over, robbed me. I was infuriated with the greedy bastard, and I was going for blood.

I made Patsy Adrianna, his cousin, come with me and drive. He was going to be there when I shot Nikki. We were getting ready to shoot Nikki when Ross stepped in. Ross was a captain in the Genovese family and president of the bread union. Nikki used to collect money for him, so Ross knew him well. He tried to intervene and protect Nikki. He thought since he worked for the Genovese family and was a bread union president, he could step in my business. He thought he'd have the power within the family to stop me. He thought wrong because we shot Nikki right on the spot.

That spiraled into the union boss getting a beating.

We gave the union boss a bullshit beating, which basically said, next time, mind your own fucking business. "No disrespect to you," I told Ross as he wiped the blood from his nose. "This situation had nothing to do with you or with your bread union. This had to do with my business. This guy stepped in my business," I said, pointing at Nikki, who was curled up on the red-stained floor. "You guys are in the wrong. I'm in the right. If that's not okay with you, then I guess me and you are going to have a situation."

"No," he replied right away, "no situation. It's not like you shot a guy around my place of business for no reason."

That's how fast things happened in the mob. Situations could get extremely violent very quickly, and one had to be fast on their feet.

CHAPTER 13

Drug Use in Gambino Family & The Kid in the Trunk

There is one thing no one ever really talked about within the five mafia crime families. It was how much the men within the mafia personally used drugs. Truth is, they sold a lot, and they used a lot. Alite was the go-to guy who held the main connections in the drug business, and the Gambino crime family would be involved with purchasing their personal cocaine through him.

John knew the formula that ran the streets. Pure and simple, it was violence and money, and he was adroit at doing both. Even though Alite could never be made because of his Albanian heritage, he had earned the full respect of the mob largely, in part, because of his ability to make large sums of money. It gave anyone the power to be respected, whether they were a made man or not. Alite was so respected that the Gambino family entrusted him to hold the old Sicilian ceremonies in the basement of his house for inducting members.

Because of Alite's uncanny ability to befriend a diversified network of hundreds of people, it allowed him the opportunity to make millions. Everyone was trying to affix themselves to him because they thought he could help them with increasing their own personal earning potential.

It would be Jo-Jo Corozzo and Ronnie "One-Arm" Trucchio who would attach themselves to John Alite. Both men had been friends since childhood and were seemingly inseparable.

I first met Ronnie One-Arm through my cousin, whom he had once dated. He was called Ronnie One-Arm because he had an accident as a child and lost the use of his arm. Ronnie had a reputation of being dangerous in his younger years from a couple shootings he did, but that's really all he did. Ronnie was not the dangerous or aggressive man people thought he was. He was only feared because of his earlier reputation.

Ronnie would become a captain for the Gambinos. He wasn't good at being able to make a dollar, mainly because he was a degenerate gambler. Therefore, Ronnie had attached himself to me because I gave him the opportunity to make money with me.

Jo-Jo and Ronnie began moving drugs with me way before either one of them became made men. The both of them had a serious appetite for cocaine; every time I turned around, they were getting high. This was the everyday norm for us. Made men were high as a kite while trying to function and run the family. These were the same fucked-up guys who never did anything yet held power, guys like Jo-Jo.

When Ronnie One-Arm had to collect money or threaten someone, he would often ask me to go along. Me helping out Ronnie was also helping Jo-Jo because most likely, it was Jo-Jo who we were strong-arming for. This would always drive Senior crazy. He'd tell me, "Don't do that shit for that fucking Jo-Jo." Gotti Senior didn't particularly care for Jo-Jo or his brother, Nicky. They didn't like Jo-Jo because he wasn't a street tough guy, but he was a money maker. Gotti looked down on people who were just money makers. Jo-Jo wasn't a tough guy never did any type of violence; he was 5'5" and 150 pounds.

It didn't stop him from getting made, though. He would become the consigliere to the Gambino family. He just wasn't a tough guy; he never did anything.

Gotti didn't like Jo-Jo's brother, Nicky Corozzo. He wasn't liked because he beat Senior with a telephone receiver as they were growing up into the mafia world. Nicky would later become the acting boss of the Gambino family. Nicky was a throwback gangster from the days of Andy Ruggiano. He was raised by Fat Andy Ruggiano, and he was straightened out by him as well.

Nicky was a gangster through and through—unlike his brother, Jo-Jo, who was a joke on the street for being in the consigliere position. He had bought his way to that position. Paid Senior to help elevate him within the mob. As we say, "He bought his button." Of course, Gotti still disliked him, but he liked his money all the way to the bank. Senior had put him on what we call the soft shake.

This was the new mob. This is what was ruining the very structure of the mafia. Situations like this where money talked louder than people's lack of ability to be a true mobster.

Jo-Jo couldn't go see Gotti Senior without having to first ask me to ask Senior if he could go see him. I would also have to ask on Jo-Jo and Nicky's behalf if they could be allowed into the club to hang out. This was yet another reason why those two men stayed close to me because they knew I had the ability and the closeness to get them near Senior.

When it came to Ronnie One-Arm, it would be Gotti Junior who didn't care for him. He'd call him, "slots" or he'd say, "Where's that fucking junkie?" Despite any disdain that might have existed between any of us, we still associated together as a tight-knit group. We understood how each of us served a purpose for the other. Junior never could grasp the dynamics of just how important it was for everyone to get along. He couldn't really comprehend anything that was going on around him, actually. I guess perhaps it was because he was Senior's kid, and he didn't have to really think."

The P.M. Pub on 101st Avenue and 84th Street in Ozone Park was the place where most of the Gambino crew would hang out, practically on a daily basis. The list of guys who today are dead is a testament to the danger and treachery that the life brought:

FRANKIE BURKE, JOEY DANIKA, KEVIN AND DENNIS PITTMAN, FAT ANGELO, ANGELO COSTELLI, DONALD, JOE O'KANE, SCOTT SCHULMAN, TITO, GREG REITER AND JOHNNY GEBERT.

The P.M. Pub was our regular hangout. We would sit there and listen to music, have a drink, play cards, and have a few laughs. It also served as our main meeting place for the drug, sports, and gambling business, along with discussions of heisting trucks or hurting guys. Everything started and stopped at the P.M. Pub.

I was fifteen minutes late for a meeting as I walked into the pub and headed to the back of the bar. I never distributed drugs in the same place very often. I kept changing the places and times where we would meet and do business. When I would buy coke, it was usually ten or fifteen kilos at a time. Once a shipment came in, I would call everybody and then let them know where we'd meet up.

When I opened the door to the ice room, Vinny Gotti, the younger brother of John and Pete Gotti, was in a heated discussion with Ronnie. He was telling him he wasn't making enough money. Vinny wasn't capable of making money either, and he depended on Ronnie to give him a piece of the action. It was almost comical because Ronnie wasn't much better than Vinny at making money. Vinny was a full-time drug user, just like the rest of the Gambino affiliates. In the mid-eighties, he would be convicted to a five-year sentence for drug sales. He had his collarbone broken by Senior Gotti for getting caught.

It didn't surprise me to find most of the guys were already high. They were always coming in high, especially Ronnie and Jo-Jo. I couldn't trust them to handle the money because they were fuck-ups. I would have to give their drugs to Tommy Crisci, who, in turn, would oversee and distribute it to them. Tommy was always on the mark with the money, but he hated being put in between Ronnie and Jo-Jo and having to keep up with them.

The heavy metal door shut behind me, making a loud thud. Everyone stopped and turned their heads. "Hey guys," I greeted as I sat my bag down of top of the steel table. I had twelve kilos of coke to distribute.

I unzipped my green duffel bag and pulled out a couple of keys. As I handed out the packages, I gave them the run down on this particular batch of drugs because every batch was different. "This is scaled stuff," I informed them. "You can hit this a little more, but listen up." I paused, making sure everyone was paying attention. "This is fish scale. This last time around, you guys had been banging it pretty good, but seriously—don't kill it."

Junior was being a fucking pain in the ass, telling me to hammer the guys for prices as I unpacked my bag. I wanted to tell him to shut the fuck up, but I still had to watch myself. My mind wandered for a split-second as I thought of the many nicknames his Uncle Vinny had for him. He would call him Baby-Bully, Kong, Urkel, and other demeaning names. No one respected him.

I had to be careful in choosing which battles were worth fighting. I was his drug partner after all, and I had to split monies with him.

When someone bad-mouthed or harassed anyone within the Gambino family, it would be my duty to step in when asked. Vito Guzzo was part of the Giannini crew, and he was out of control and wild. He was becoming more aggressive not only with Junior, but with other Gambino members. He and his crew were robbing and killing like crazy. They were doing some really bad crimes, hurting women, doing armed robberies, and killing their own friends.

He thought he was smart, but he was a dummy, and he sounded like one if you heard him talk. I'd known Vito since I was a kid. We stayed in touch with each other here and there, but we never consistently hung out together. He had a brother who went to prison for a double homicide during a drug deal. His father had stayed around the Colombo family and would later be murdered.

Vito Guzzo's friends had started bothering Patsy Conte at his club. Patsy was a captain in the Gambino family. He owned Key

Food Supermarkets and a typical Italian social club. Patsy Conte was also involved with the infamous Pizza Connection. The Pizza Connection dealt in large amounts of heroin, cocaine, and any other pill or drug they could sell. The business generated tens of millions of dollars in profits, all the while using a network of pizza restaurants as a front. It was a huge drug ring operation that stretched from Italy to the United States, and it came after the French connection cases of the '70s.

Patsy went to Junior and asked him to do something about Vito and his friends. I think Vito's crew was still wanting revenge over Patsy's nephew having shot Vito Guzzo. Patsy would later serve time when his very own brother would testify against him.

Vito was merely warned to stop fucking around with Patsy, or he was going to have problems. I knew a simple warning wouldn't be enough to stop him. There was only one thing men like Vito understood, and that was violence.

Vito, of course, ignored his warning and was right back at bothering Patsy at his club. I happened to be out of town that weekend, so Junior had to take care of the situation. Unfortunately, he didn't have any capable guys or friends of his own, especially guys who were capable of handling Vito. Not having anyone to call on, Junior was in a pinch. He wound up calling the guys on my own personal crew for help. He called my cousin, Pat, Michael, and a couple other guys to go to the club and confront Vito's guys.

The only one of Junior's guys who went to give backup was Frank Radice. It would be several more years before Frank Radice would become a made guy for the Gambino family. Frank's brother John was a convicted heroin dealer whose daughter would end up marrying into the Gotti family. It would be Junior's brother Peter who would have a son and name him Johnny.

Johnny wound up for going to prison for illegal drug sales, caught working out of his very own grandfather's house, whose wife still lived there.

He had three cases stacked against him at once. He was caught talking on old tapes with his big-mouth talk, but changed his tune in court, crying, "I'm a drug addict." It was all rhetoric.

His final sentence was only eight years in prison.

What he did was impossible. He had three separate felony charges, not one in the same case, and for the number of drugs he was selling, eight years was a slap on the wrist. Everyone knows he talked in order to get a reduced sentence.

When my guys got to Patsy's Club, they had a small scuffle. In the end, my guys wound up getting a hold of Paulie Ragusa, who was one of Vito's men. We informed Junior that we didn't have Vito, but we had Paulie. Junior ordered us to baseball bat Paulie to a pulp, and so we did.

Ragusa would, years later, go to jail for an armored car robbery and for a shoot-out with the police. He ended up in Ray Brook prison at the same time Junior was there serving time. He stayed with Junior, even after knowing it was Junior who had my guys baseball bat him. I lost a lot of respect for the mafia that day.

Ironically, that type of scene was the same old mafia bullshit. Everything was a joke, and that was part of the treachery of the mob. It was comprised of fake friends with no backbone and no loyalty. I had to keep an eye on my own friends because brother-type trust was hard to come by. I had to stay five steps ahead of everyone, constantly on the look-out for the upcoming pitfalls of lies, deception, and trickery.

This incident had tensions rising, and it took me to the next level with Vito, and not in a good way. Keep your friends close and your enemies closer. This was the relationship Vito and I would soon find ourselves in. Relationships were always being strained and pushed to limits, and it didn't help that Junior was instigating issues between Vito, myself, and his entire crew. I didn't need to know Junior was manipulating me. I didn't care, but I was in a position where I worked for the Gambino family. I had to play along and put up with him creating unnecessary tensions and had to deal with it strategically. It was like having to dance on a tight rope.

Vito was continually challenging Junior, testing the waters to see what Junior was about. Junior would do nothing about his advances, so Vito would see for himself that Junior had no balls, and that was going to be a big problem. Vito pushed further, stirring up trouble in other establishments where our guys would sometimes hang out.

I happened to be in the same club Vito was in one night. We were at the Lemon Tree, a hot club on Austin Street in Kew Gardens, and one of Vito's guys started causing problems, harassing Frankie Radice. One of Frankie's friends had come upstairs to get me, asking me to step in.

I headed downstairs and stopped in the narrow hallway behind the kid who was mouthing off. His name was Bobby, and he, like Vito, was gaining confidence, thinking he could run roughshod over a made man and get away with it. He thought wrong.

When I hit the last step, Bobby turned to me and boldly said, "All of Junior's guys got no balls, none of them. They're fucking punks with big mouths." He wasn't going to stop talking. "They only got balls if you're around."

Bobby was in great shape and good-looking. He wasn't a gangster or a tough guy, and he was too stupid to know he was skating on thin ice. He didn't realize what I could do to him.

"Come upstairs," I told him. "Let's get out of the hallway and talk about this."

He agreed and then followed me up the stairs, along with the others. When I got to a quiet spot where the music wasn't blaring, I turned around and told Bobby sternly, "I can't let you talk about our guys like this."

"Well, they're only tough if you're here," he said fearlessly. Bobby wouldn't stop mouthing off, and I had given him his one warning. I looked over at Frankie with a look in my eye that told him how disgusted I was with this kid.

"And you know what, John?" Bobby added. "You're the only one who's got balls here. Only you and your guys have balls. Gotti's guys are fucking faking at being tough." My facial expressions remained neutral, but on the inside, I had already planned my next step.

He then started telling me about what Vito thought about Gotti and how he was telling everyone Gotti's guys were all full of shit. I glanced over at my friend Michael Finnerty and gave a slight nod. The kid thinks he has my ear because he was kissing my ass. He had another thing coming.

I broke into the conversation and suggested we go somewhere else to talk about this. "Let's go for a walk," I said in a friendly voice that masked my true intentions.

He must have thought it a cool thing to think he was going to hang out with me and Michael because he agreed easily. Mike and I walked outside with him. As we strolled down the street, we talked to him. He was a dumb kid, not really sharp. He thought he was somebody because he was hanging out with Vito. We turned the corner of the club and then stopped in front of a McDonald's, where my car was parked.

"Get in the car," I told him. It was at this point, his entire demeanor changed. Maybe it was the tone of my voice or the look in my eye, but I could tell by his body language that he just realized something wasn't right. In the next moment, he turned and tried to take off, but Michael and I were too quick and jumped him. My intentions were to throw him in the trunk of the car and hold him captive because I was going to kill him.

He was extremely strong in his struggling to break free. He was panicking, floundering like a fish out of water. He put up a good fight because Michael and I were having a hell of a time wrestling him into the trunk of my car. There was a lot of kicking, twisting of bodies, grunts, and cursing. It's not as easy to get a guy in the trunk like everybody thinks it would be. The movies portray it to look simple and effortless.

We had him halfway into the trunk when a cop showed up. "What's going on here?" he asked, his eyes narrowed.

Immediately, we let go of Bobby. He popped out of the trunk and stood straight, holding out his palms, quickly explaining, "It's all good, officer. We were just playing around."

"You sure about that?" the cop asked, keeping his hand near his holster.

"They weren't doing anything but horsing around with me," he reassured.

The cop pulled me aside and asked for my identification. He knew who I was, everybody knew who I was, but I gave it to him anyway. He looked at my license, then handed it back. He gave me a look of uncertainty before he turned to the kid and asked, "Are you sure you're all right?"

"I'm good," he assured the policeman.

I gave Bobby a friendly hug, then shook his hand. "We'll be talking," I told him with a light smile. He was trying to contain his shaking in fear. He was scared, nervous, and full of too many other emotions to count.

"Okay, John," he said, "but I don't want no problem like that."

I watched as he left down the sidewalk. He was heading back toward the bar, and I knew he was going straight to Vito. These types of incidents were constant, all because of Junior. He was too stupid to understand what he initiated. Even Vito would be too dumb to see the whole picture because he wound up shooting Angelo Ruggiero's younger son, Louis. Vito did a stupid thing for a stupid reason. One just doesn't shoot Gotti Senior's right-hand man's son and expect to get away with it. He was probably drinking, had a couple words over something, and then lost his temper. I don't know if Vito knew it was Angelo's son or not. Not sure he would've cared.

I wanted to tell Vito that it was him who was putting his own guys on the hook and that he was creating bad friction between his crews and ours. In the mob world, there had to be something done, and that meant it would fall to me to be the enforcer.

CHAPTER 14

Joe & Vito Steal Money

Alite's best friends, his real and true friends, were guys who were not part of the mafia life. They were a handful of regular, everyday nice guys John knew since he was six years old. There was an unspoken bond between all of them, and they knew John would kill for them at the drop of a hat. If anyone attempted to hurt them or anyone in their families, they would never say anything to John. They would work things out themselves. If they had a problem, they kept quiet because they were true friends protecting John in their own way.

When it came to my crew, it was my obligation to protect them like a wallet. Ninety-nine percent of my crew were not shooters, and in reality, if they couldn't shoot, they were liabilities. I would have been naïve to think otherwise.

I also had business partners and other associations to consider. The problem was, I was genuine to my friends, crew, and associations. I liked them all, actually, but most of them only stayed with me for protection and the ability to make money. I had to be careful. I would forget sometimes I couldn't be nice to these guys the way I was to my closest friends. Some were good-hearted guys, but they were not my good friends. They had hidden motives and their own agendas.

These men were in the game, as long as we were going through good times. The majority of my crew and associates, every single weakness you showed them, they'd turn it around and bite you on the ass like a snake—even in my times of need.

There is an old story that typifies the treachery of the mafia life.

Once upon a time, there was man who came upon an injured snake. This man carefully attended to the snake's wounds, protected him, and healed him. The moment the snake was cured, he bit the man.

"I am about to die," the man cried out in disbelief and shock. "Why did you do that?" The man had really cared for the snake like a friend. The deadly bite was the last thing he had been expecting.

"Because I'm a snake; what did you think I was going to do?" he hissed.

As the man lay dying, he cried out in agony, "How could you do this to me? You promised not to bite me! I did everything for you! I trusted you!"

"You knew what I was when you picked me up," he scoffed. "What did you think I'd do? I'm a snake; it's who I am," the snake replied, slithering away, leaving the man to die.

The main issue I was dealing with at the time was the fact that I lived by my own set of rules and ethics. I'd sworn long ago I would never kill my best friends. I just had something inside me that came from deep within, the unspoken brotherhood we had since we were young kids. I wouldn't kill anyone from my crew or other associates whom I considered friends, either. Even when they would do me wrong, I wouldn't take their life. That was a line I would never cross while living in this world, mafia-related or not. But sparing certain lives would sometimes come back to haunt me.

Joe O'Kane was someone I had considered one of those good friends, and he was part of my crew. I basically raised him since he was a kid and taught him how to be streetwise. Joe had a weasel side that I saw from day one, and I knew he was a weak-minded snake in the grass. I took him under my wing and protected him. I helped him because I genuinely liked his parents, his sisters Fran and Marie, and his little niece, who was adorable.

I doled out many beatings to tough guys I knew, just for harassing Joe. I remembered when Joe got shot in his legs earlier in life. I went after the guy who shot him. The guy left the country, and I chased him all the way into Italy. Joe also got slapped around once by Johnny Gebert, and so I beat Johnny up for it, and at the time, he was actually a friend of mine.

I had taken Joe O'Kane with me to Florida, Mexico, and, on several occasions, California. He would stay with me in Beverly Hills. I had kept in contact over the years with an ex-girlfriend who resembled Kelly McGillis. Her name was Kate Conway, and her father was an original New Yorker, which gave her an attachment to me. She was from a wealthy family, and she was classy. Kate wanted to introduce her girlfriend, who was visiting from Italy. She, also, was wealthy and classy. Joe O'Kane was with me on that trip and was introduced to Kate's girlfriend. It was a mess. He had worn a track suit with about twenty gold chains slung around his neck. He had four or five large and obnoxious rings on. I had warned him to dress with some class and tone his shit down, but he wouldn't.

When we went to Kate's apartment, Joe pulled me aside. He told me he pissed on her toothbrush while in her bathroom and then put it back in its holder. I flipped out. "You are a low-life piece of shit," I yelled, then slapped him hard across the face. "Don't you ever disrespect my friends." I slapped him again, and he broke into tears, apologizing profusely.

So that was his personality—a coward and a spiteful piece of shit. Anyone from the streets could read right through him in a heartbeat. He had no loyalty to anything but the dollar. He was extremely cheap and, just like the wind, he would drift where the power was, or where he could make more money. He would snake his own mother for a dollar, and that was no hidden secret in my neighborhood. Despite his shortcomings, I had kept Joe around for business reasons.

Even though I held him at a further distance now, I would still have to pull him out of trouble from time to time. He could never handle his own business, and he'd tell people he was my best friend so he could maneuver through the streets. He used my name for everything, including making relationships with guys like Vito Guzzo.

Joe and Vito had gotten friendly with each other pretty quickly. They bought a strip club in New York together called Naked City. Joe thought he was getting big and started to push the limits with me and everyone else. He thought he was smarter than Junior, smarter than everybody. He just kept playing guys and using them, but he couldn't use or outsmart me. Not on his best day.

I found out Joe and Vito were doing a fair amount of business together behind my back. It wasn't until Vito started doing business with Joe that I began to have my own personal problems with Vito.

Joe was making moves within the coke business and not paying me. I couldn't let him get away with that. I needed to send a clear message to Joe.

Both Steve and George Catalano were working for me at the time, so I sent them over to Joe's place to rob and beat him up. I specifically told them to hurt him good, but not to stab or shoot him. I knew the Catalano brothers hated him and would've loved to have seen him dead. One of the brothers wound up taking the beating a bit further and stabbed Joe.

I always had a sixth sense when things were off, and everything was pointed at Joe. I was always able to stay a few steps ahead of everyone. I had my own network of guys who were involved with other crime factions, but they were loyal to me. The moment Joe and

Vito met up, I put feelers out there. I wanted to keep a close eye on them.

Pinto was one of my guys who used to answer the phones in my bookmaking office. Pinto talked with different crews and gangs, keeping me up-to-date on anything important. He was familiar with everyone and had built his own informational network as well.

Pinto told me Joe was sneaking around, trying to get into business with as many guys as possible. I knew he had been doing business with Vito, but he just signed on with Keith Pellegrino, who was part of my own personal crew. If I were any other mobster, I would've killed them all by now for doing business outside of me and behind my back. They all knew better.

Joe already got stabbed up for making moves within the coke business and not paying me. It wasn't the first time we had to rob and beat him up for not doing what he was supposed to do.

Pinto had come to me a couple days before to let me know Anthony Tabbita was spending a lot of money. Pinto thought something was off. He had been doing quite a bit of gambling through my sports business, which was nothing new, but it was the way he was gambling that threw up a red flag.

Pinto had gotten word through a network of friends that somehow Vito was going to try and hit me, using Joe O'Kane, who would set it up. This wasn't really a surprise. After all, he had set up his best friend, Joey Stabile, to be murdered. My entire life, I'd been protecting Joe from others who wanted him dead, and now he wants me killed.

Pinto told me in detail what their plot was. It was Anthony Tabbita who worked for Vito Guzzo, and he was part of the set up. If he won, Pinto was going to be the one to go pay him. The amount of money he was betting, he didn't have it to lose. He couldn't cover that bet. Him losing would then require me to make a personal visit.

He was trying to lose on purpose so I would have to go see him. He was going to try and make me meet him somewhere, and it would be at that chosen spot where they were going to kill me.

It wouldn't be the first time, nor the last time that somebody wanted me dead. I didn't tell Gotti Senior very often when someone tried to hit me. What he cared about was the amount of heat I was constantly bringing to him and the crew.

I was always getting myself into both personal and business trouble, and I was warned over and over by Gotti Senior to slow down, or I'd be the one getting killed by my own people. He told me that hundreds of times. I could hear him screaming at me now, "Stop bringing so much heat to us. Stop bringing so much trouble. Stop shooting everybody unless it's on a direct order from me." If I had been just another soldier to him, he probably would've had me killed, but he treated me like family.

Vito and his crew were extremely violent. One day, he would find himself being on America's Most Wanted television show, along with some of his guys. The rest would later end up ratting on me. That was the street; it was garbage and shit, through and through.

My mind was spinning, jumping with a million thoughts all at once. My mind was on Ronnie One-Arm. I had to wonder if Ronnie knew Vito and his guys were trying to hit me. Ronnie had grown up with Vito Guzzo's older brother, and they stayed pretty tight. I was certain Guzzo's brother would've told Ronnie.

Thousands of us were all so closely connected and intertwined. Whether it be friend of a friend, business relations, or marriage, all of us had personal connections amongst each other. Because of the matrix of people, I believed it created confusion as to where one's loyalties should be. People would forget what side they were on.

Prior to me, Ronnie One-Arm told everybody he was Robert Ingles's partner. Robert Ingles was known as a big-time fucking shooter for the Gambino family, and to this day, he remains my friend. Ronnie used him, attached himself to him as his partner, and then when Robert wasn't around anymore, Ronnie then attached himself to me. I had known Ronnie long enough to know he was a pussy, and he played all angles, but we were supposed to be good friends.

If it weren't for me, Ronnie never would've been made. When it came to me discussing with Senior about Ronnie getting made, it was Junior Gotti and Bobby Boriello who had asked me to knock it down. They were trying to give me orders. They wanted me to tell Senior not to have Ronnie One-Arm made.

I wouldn't do it—I wouldn't tell Senior what they wanted me to. I stood up for him, and he got made because of my recommendation to Senior. He was a friend, and I was there for him when he needed me. I made him big money, protected him, just like Joe O'Kane.

My mind jumped from one man to the next. I would deal with Ronnie later. I had to focus on planning my strategy and decide how I was going to handle Keith Pellegrino, Joe O'Kane, and Vito Guzzo. I would take swift action before Joe and Vito could know what hit them.

I already knew Joe's day-to-day patterns. He would work out with Vito at World's Gym on a constant basis. Vito would pick him up, and when he'd drop him off, he would stay and usually hang out in Joe's apartment for a while.

It wouldn't have mattered if I owned the apartment building Joe was living in or not. If I wanted someone, nothing was going to stop me from getting to them. It just so happened, however, that I was the owner of the apartment building where Joe was living. He was renting my top-floor apartment.

I had no intentions of killing Joe, and that was the major difference between us. Despite Joe having no loyalty and being able to set up hits on his own friends, I was never going to kill him or have him killed. I was just going to scare the shit out of him, tie him up, and then I was going to take him somewhere in the middle of nowhere. I'd just leave him to think I was going to leave him there to die.

I was, however, going to kill Vito Guzzo.

CHAPTER 15

The Hit (Joe, Keith, & Vito)

Plenty of thought and planning went into a hit like this one. Alite, a master at planning his next moves and his hits, didn't just show up with a gun and clip the guy.

I had brought several guys in on the hit with me. One of them was my brother-in-law, Pat. Then I had Kevin Bonner, who hated Joe and blamed Joe for the death of his brother.

Joe had stepped in and married his girl, and then later had a baby with her.

Kevin and I had a history that went way back. He was tough. I remembered the time we baseball batted two guys together. After we beat them, Kevin tied one to his car while I wrapped a wire around the other's neck, then tied him to my bumper. We both drove away, dragging them behind our cars.

I had parked a van around the back of the apartment complex and laid plastic sheets out on the floor in the hallway downstairs. The Catalano brothers were already in the building, ready and waiting. Joey Miaoli served as the lookout man. He was sitting in his car and was staked out in front of the building with a handheld radio.

Taking over Joe's apartment was easy. One of Joe's friends had been relaxing on the sofa when we broke in. He didn't put up a fight. All we had to do was grab him, then tie him up in the back room. As I was tying him up, I reassured him that I wasn't going to kill him.

I said, "I'm not going to gag you, but you're going to stay here and shut your mouth." I leaned in close to drive my point home. "If you make one tiny peep back here, you're going to force me to take you somewhere and then kill you," I said in all seriousness. "I don't want to do that because this matter doesn't concern you. Do you understand what I'm saying?" The kid was shaking and speechless, but he nodded his head like a bobblehead doll to tell me he understood.

We began to set up and get things in place. I had put Kevin Bonner in the bathroom, my brother-in-law and Phil Barone's son, Phil Junior, who was an MMA fighter, in the hall closet. Maybe fifteen minutes had gone by before Joey radioed me, letting me know that Joe was on his way up.

When Joe walked in, he found me casually sitting on the couch as if I were just hanging out.

"Hey, John," he greeted with a curious lilt, wondering what I was doing here. He closed the door behind him, unaware of what was about to unfold. "So, what brings you by?" he asked as he turned away from the entrance and came toward me.

I slipped the nine-millimeter out from underneath the pillow and then pointed it at him. "Get on the floor," I said coldly.

He immediately started to cry as he fell to his knees. "You have balls," I growled. I got up from the sofa and stepped closer. "Were you trying to set me up for them to kill me?" I demanded to know.

"John, please," he begged through his pitiful tears. He was trembling. My guys stepped out from hiding, and then Joe's glassy eyes grew wide with terror. I set the gun down, retrieved my rope, and then proceeded to tie him up.

"You know why everyone always wondered why I kept you around?" I asked, slipping the rope around his wrists.

He shook his head, afraid to speak.

"I'll tell you what I told them," I said, leaning in closer as I tied a knot, over-tightening it. "He's like dog shit, making money all over the place, and I thought I could control him. I knew what he was, I told them, but I thought he was just my loyal fucking piece of dog shit," I shouted angrily. I could feel my face getting red with anger.

He simply got too cocky, even with me. He was a greedy weasel, and he thought he could maneuver everyone.

Junior had abused Joe his entire life, and he always asked me why I was keeping the piece of shit around. So even though Gotti Junior could never stand Joe, lately, Junior was befriending him. Junior's ulterior motive to hang out with Joe was to get closer to him in order to get closer to Vito Guzzo in order to set him up. Joe, of course, was too stupid to realize what was going on. He never understood the life.

The only thing Joe was trying to do by hanging out with Vito, Junior, and Ronnie One-Arm was to see if any one of them could get me to stop robbing and hurting him. He thought he'd have a measure of protection under these guys, but he didn't.

"Were you paying Vito off with your own money to have me hit?"

"No, I promise," he quickly answered. I wasn't totally convinced.

"Okay, Joe, how much money do you have?"

"John—I swear," he said with conviction, "I'm broke. I don't have anything."

I scoffed because I knew he was doing a serious amount of business with Vito. Joe beat me for a lot of money and then set me up. "My entire life, I've been protecting you. I took you in under my wing so you could make more money than you ever dreamed, and this is how you thank me?" I roared.

"I don't have any money, John!" he cried out.

"Is that right?" I mocked as I stood straight. I had a special radio, and when dialed to a certain frequency, I could make a phone call to anyone. I picked up the radio and slowly punched in the numbers on the phone. Glancing down at Joe, I asked, "I'm going to ask you again, Joe. How much do you have?"

He chose to remain silent while trying to control his tears. "Well, I happen to know what you have," I said. "There's two bank accounts and two safety deposit boxes in your name. Just to verify I'm wrong, let's call the bank, shall we?" As soon as the phone rang, I held the radio out in front of him so he could speak. I gave him a hard glare. "You're going to ask them to give you the balances of all the accounts you have."

The bank Joe was doing business with just so happened to be the bank where Phil Barone's aunt worked. Joe had no clue the lady on the other line was Phil's aunt and that she was in on the scheme. Joe gave her the credentials needed in order to access his accounts.

"You've got six hundred thousand in your account, and in the other, you have two hundred thousand dollars," she informed us through the speaker, then added, "Plus, you have two safety deposit boxes."

I didn't know what he held in those boxes, but we all knew he was good for at least a million dollars. I disconnected the call and asked him, "How much is your life worth now?"

"Please, John, don't kill me," he begged. He was shaking in fear. I ignored him, as I was on to the next step, which was to call Keith Pellegrino.

As I dialed his number, I told Joe what he was going to say to him. "You're going to tell Keith you need to see him right away. Don't tell him what's wrong, just say you need him to come over and that you can't discuss it over the phone." Keith lived only a couple of blocks away, so it would take less than five minutes for him to get there.

The second he strolled through the door, my men surrounded him. "Get on the floor," I said, holding him at gunpoint.

His eyes shifted nervously from one man to the next as Keith slowly knelt on the carpeted floor beside Joe. These guys had known me since I was a kid. Keith's daughter, Nicole, was my godchild. I couldn't believe it.

I glanced between both men and said, "You're both cocksuckers. I should kill both of you right now. You low-level pieces of shit. I kept you safe over the years while helping you earn money." I really wanted to kill them, but it was because of both of their families that I held up. They all had become friends with me. I tried to keep a different set of rules than most guys because anybody else would've killed them before now. "You both are weaklings, always having to use my name so you can maneuver in the streets."

I was pissed off and wired up. They'd seen me in this mode every day—they just never had such a high level of my anger directed at them. They were scared. They betrayed me, and they knew how ruthless I was in these situations. Both of them knelt before me, crying like babies as tears streamed down their cheeks. I could smell their fear.

"You're the same man I helped to survive the streets. You grow up around me, and I'm making you a shit ton of money—and you thought you could pull one over on me? I helped open up tons of businesses with you, but you never would do the right thing back." He never reciprocated. "You couldn't stand on your own two feet in the drug business, or in the street, without me." He wasn't a tough guy or a shooter. He was weak and stupid. He had done some armed robberies with me, but he always waited outside.

"So if you think the both of you are so tough, then why aren't you taking care of your own business? Why am I shooting guys and baseball batting guys for you? You both were out sneaking behind me, making your own alliances while robbing me. Why are you then running to me when the heat is yours?"

Not giving a shit about anyone's tears, I took a quick step forward with the gun, and Keith flinched hard. He thought I was going to shoot him, but I had flipped the gun around, offering it to him. "Here's my gun, Keith. Will you kill your friend Joe here if I tell you to?" I asked, jerking my chin in Joe's direction. "Show everyone here what a lowlife you are. Would you do it?"

"Yes," he sobbed. "Yes."

One thing is for certain: when guys are put in this type of position, they'll sell each other out in a heartbeat. I see it all the time. There was no friendship in either one of these guys—there never was. They were just greedy fucks, and money trumped all. I already knew that Keith would've killed Joe in order to save his own life.

"No, please, no," Joe begged, looking at Keith in horror.

I took the gun away from Keith, then stepped in front of Joe. "Don't worry, Joe, I'm not going to kill you like that." I leaned down close to his face and said in a deep, gravelly voice, "I'm not going to put a finger on you. I'm going to put you in a fucking hole, and I'm going to let you die just like that. No water, no bathroom, no nothing. You're going to sit there for fucking days until you die." The deadness in my eyes told him I would.

I grabbed the radio again and started dialing Vito's number. All of us expected him to have come up to Joe's apartment, but for whatever reason, he didn't.

"We're calling Vito, and you're going to tell him you need to talk to him in person or that he forgot something," I told Joe. "You're going to be convincing," I said in a voice that said if he screwed up, there would be bad consequences.

The phone rang twice, then Vito answered. "Hey, Vito," Joe greeted. Keeping his voice calm and even, he asked, "Hey, can you come back to the house?"

"No, I can't right now," Vito replied.

"I really need to speak with you," Joe pleaded.

"I gotta go somewhere. It's important, but I'll call you later." It was obvious Vito wasn't going to come back to the apartment. Vito got very lucky that day.

There would be another time I'd set up Vito to be killed, but my guys would screw it up. They would shoot him five times, but they would make the mistake of not making sure he was dead. Vito survived the attempted murder.

"This is what we're going to do," I said, looking at Keith. "You're going to go to Joe's mother's house to get whatever money he's got there and bring it back here." He nodded his head. "Don't screw this up."

"I promise, I won't," Keith assured. We let Keith leave. He had returned a half-hour later. When he walked into Joe's apartment, he had a duffel bag slung over his shoulder.

"There was only twenty-five thousand stashed there," he said, holding out the bag.

"Okay." I pulled the bag from his hands, then turned around, handing the duffel bag to Kevin. "Here you go. Split this up with each other. I don't want any of it."

Kevin Bonner would later testify to this very scene in court. He would say, "John Alite didn't do it for the money." It was true—I didn't need the money, I was loaded.

I walked over to Joe, who was still tied up on the floor with his hands behind his back. "This was an example," I said angrily. "I could kill you now. Just who do you think you're fucking with?" I yelled.

"Please don't kill me," Joe cried.

"The only reason why I don't kill you is because I like your family."

After that incident, Joe, of course, went right back to Vito to tell him everything.

Because of my friendship with Pinto, I knew these guys had several plots to kill me. Joe was not only setting up my hits, but he was setting up others' as well. Vito's crew had attempted to hit me several times. Once near the Aqueduct racetrack, at my home in Jersey, and another time chasing me with a van.

So these guys can't kill me. They don't know how to kill me. They're all afraid to kill me, but they're all plotting to kill me. They were all sneaking around because they weren't going to hit me themselves. They were trying to make angles to get someone to hit me because those guys never did anything. It was just like Ronnie One-Arm did with Scott Schulman. He hired out instead of being a tough guy.

These guys were all talk because they didn't even know how to set up a hit. They were too stupid to get away with the crime. Their hesitation and fear allowed me to stay one step ahead of them. For the average person, the hard part for them was pulling the trigger. That was the absolute easiest part for me. The hard part, I always told everybody, was being able to get away with the crime afterward.

There was nobody stopping me from doing anything. Even Ronnie One-Arm would go to Anthony Ruggiano, who was Fat Andy's son. Ronnie knew I was friendly with the Ruggiano family, and he asked Anthony if he could slow me down from hurting and robbing all these guys. It was obvious the mob couldn't control me because I was doing whatever I wanted, and nobody was doing anything about it.

No one could protect anybody from me if I wanted them, not even Junior. I baseball batted, stabbed, and almost killed Richard Gotti's son-in-law on the side of the Belt Parkway. I beat up Junior's uncle in prison and robbed his bookmaker. I robbed Ronnie One-Arm and his bookmaker twice. I had one instance after another, and nobody did anything about it.

Before I left the apartment, I got onto Joe for not paying Ronnie One-Arm the five hundred dollars a week he owed him. He told me he didn't want to pay Ronnie but that he'd give me the money instead.

"Those days are over, you seeing me," I said in a heated tone. "Now you've fucked yourself. So you'd better start paying them; otherwise, they're going to want me to hurt you."

Everybody always pushed the boundaries, their greed driving them over the edge. In one way or another, it would always catch up with them. Sometimes gluttony would be their very demise. When someone screwed me over or beat me for a lot of money, they could rest assured that no matter how many years would go by, I was never going to forget. I was merely waiting for the right opportunity to present itself.

When Ronnie One-Arm lost money to me and my father's book-making office, he tried to stiff us. He owed my father almost nine thousand dollars and would only pay him four thousand. I was in jail at the time when my father told me. I told my dad, "Just take the four thousand, and don't worry about the rest. When I come home, I'll take care of it."

I thought to myself, "Who the fuck do they think they're fucking with? When I come home, I'm just going to get even." This was another problem with the loyalty of the mob. When you're gone, you're gone. When you're in jail, it's like a free-for-all.

When I came home from jail, first thing I did within the first week was I robbed Ronnie One-Arm. I actually robbed one of Ronnie One-Arm's bookmakers in Valley Stream. Steve Cadillano and Johnny Burke were with me. I'd known Johnny since we were kids. (No relation to Frankie Burke). Johnny hid behind a wall while Steve stayed as the lookout man around the corner.

I walked into the bookmaker's office and beat the guy up. He was about six foot five inches and weighed three hundred pounds, but that didn't bother me. I beat him up, wrestled him to the ground, then tied him up. I robbed him of about six thousand dollars and took his expensive watch.

"Do you know whose place this is?" he said, trying to catch his breath from the struggle.

"You don't think I don't know whose place I'm in? You think I could give a shit?" I grabbed a piece of scrap paper and wrote my name down with an ink pen. Standing before him, I crumbled the paper into a ball. "You can tell him it was me," I said as I shoved the paper into his mouth and taped his mouth shut.

The second thing I did was meet with Ronnie One-Arm. We met at a train station. His son, who was recently straightened out, was tagging along. The kid had no idea about the mob—that's how dumb Ronnie was. He stupidly involved his son in the mob.

I verbally abused Ronnie for bringing his son along. Ronnie then asked his son to go inside the station because he didn't want his son to hear what I was going to say.

"First off," I said to Ronnie. "I sold the watch, so you're not getting it back." Meanwhile, I was wearing, a t-shirt so he could plainly see it on my wrist.

I said to him, "Not only did I rob your bookmaker, but then I robbed a drug dealer, Sean Dunn. And the Gotti's son-in-law. After I hurt Gotti's son-in-law, I took money off him, too."

Later, Kevin Bonner would receive a twenty-seven-year sentence and then become a witness against all of the Gotti crew.

Like Kevin, Keith Pellegrino would prove to be yet another lifelong friend who would betray Alite and cooperate with the authorities. Not only did he tell on the first shooting John did in 1988, but he said that John actually had his car when he shot a guy named Paul. John made Keith a lot of money, but typically, people of the street don't ever recip-rocate. Keith never helped anybody, and he always had his hand out for help. John expands on the story:

At Keith's hearing, I would discover that he withheld the infor-mation that him and Chris Tarantino were involved in the murder of Greg Reiter. Keith had gone into the gym business with me, but he had also opened up different gyms with Chris Tarantino. Chris would one day serve a life sentence for three or four murders, one of them being of his good friend, and for killing an armored car driver.

Had I known that Keith Pellegrino was part of Greg's demise, I would've killed him in a second. I wanted blood, but the Gottis stopped me from taking Keith out.

I now fully understood that Joe O'Kane, Vito, and Ronnie One-Arm were all involved in a plot to kill me. In other words, for that to have happened, John Gotti Junior had to be part of it so he could approve it. He knew that Ronnie One-Arm knew they were going to try to kill me, and it was okayed.

Most of these guys were snakes, except Tabbita and Fabbi. As far as Vito goes, I only respected him as my enemy. He was gangster and was dangerous. Anthony Tabbita, Fabbi, and I wound up becoming good friends and are still friends today. They never agreed with some of Vito's crimes and walked away from him, starting their new life in a positive way.

Anthony Tabbita

BONUS CHAPTER

TT / RAP

My name is Jay Tee Spurgeon. Not many call me by my real name. I'm known on the street as TT. My name was known all over as being one of the biggest drug dealers in Brooklyn and parts of New York since the late '70s. I didn't have customers or a crew, per se. I basically ran by myself and did my own thing. I was one of the fortunate few to be able to sell full kilos at a time and not have to deal with the smaller distributions. Back in my day, I could buy a kilo for fourteen thousand dollars, then cook it. I would then turn it around and sell it to a guy in North Carolina for thirty-two thousand dollars, more than doubling my money. I used to leave my house with a roll of quarters for the payphone, and I'd come back home with twenty to forty thousand dollars, easy. It was so easy. I was young, and I was filthy rich, and people didn't mess with me anymore.

I was first introduced to John Alite through a mutual friend of ours, Charles Carneglia. Charles and I didn't do business together; we were just good friends. We both frequented a place in Brooklyn called the Lindenwood Diner.

I can't remember exactly where John and I met because it was so long ago, but the very moment we did, we hit it off immediately. I think the reason why we bonded so quickly was because we had so much in common.

I grew up on the streets the same way John did. I used to be five-seven and one hundred thirty pounds. I was a little guy with a skinny physique, but I could pack a mean punch. We both grew up poor, learned how to fight with our hands, and we were the guys in our own school who fought all the bullies—all of them. I couldn't stand bullies. I was a child of nine and had to fend for myself a lot. My mother was legally blind and a single parent. She did the best she could for us, and I don't fault her for anything. My mother tried to

teach me in my formative years to walk a straight path, but when I had reached a certain age, I chose to go the wrong way.

Being half-Spanish and half-black wasn't an easy road for me at first. I had to put in a lot of work when I was on the street level in order to prove myself and earn respect. I wasn't a troublemaker, but I also was not somebody you wanted to mess with. I wouldn't tolerate anything that could pose a threat to me on the streets. If I did, I would've been trampled over. It took me years, but I earned my marks. I did a lot of foolish things in my past, but at the end of the day, what was important to me then was that people knew who I was.

As I grew older, I started making more and more money, and there was no way I was going to leave the streets. It's a fact: once the streets get a hold of you, they got you. I could see me having all the best things in life. The things I couldn't have as a child growing up, like having the best sneakers. Those type of things were what I wanted because I couldn't have them as a kid. I wanted to wear the best clothes, drive the best cars, I wanted the best women, the best vacations. My list was never ending.

When I would go to the more prestigious clubs in town, I couldn't let anyone show me up. If someone was on the other side of a bar from me and I would see them buying three bottles of expensive champagne, I wouldn't let them outdo me. I would order ten or fifteen bottles of champagne. It was all about status and flamboyance for me, as if the more champagne one bought, the bigger they were in the eyes of the public.

There was an unspoken, mutual respect me and John had for each other right off. Part of the reason we had respect for each other was that we knew what it took to get to the status level we were operating at. We broke through the crowd and made names for ourselves. We rose out of poverty by ourselves. We also had the intellect, capability, drive, and determination to build our own empires. Not many held all those attributes to be successful like me and John.

I will never forget the first time John went out with me for lunch. He had me meet him at an Irish pub in Ozone Park. Being a small guy with my size and ethnic background, I felt a little uncomfortable sitting around in an all-white bar.

"I can't believe you got me in this freaking white, Irish bar, man," I complained, pretending to be irritated.

John knew I was messing with him because he cracked a grin, and we laughed. I took a seat at the bar to place an order while John ventured to the other side of the bar to say hello to someone. A minute after John had stepped away, an Irish guy approached me. He was a really big guy, a monster, was probably a little drunk, and he said some things to me that he shouldn't have. At this point in my life, I had become less reactionary and more calm and mature. I was thinking how to handle this in a more civilized manner, but John saw the look on my face before I could recover my shocked expression.

In two long strides, John was at his back. He grabbed his shoulder and nudged him out of the way to stand between us. He looked from the Irish guy, then to me. "What the fuck did he say to you?" he asked in his deep, gravelly voice.

I looked at John and said, "He asked me what the fuck I was doing in this bar. He was talking to me like I shouldn't be in here at all."

I didn't even have time to blink before John had punched the guy so hard, he stumbled backward. Then John just pounded him again and again. They guy dropped to the floor and curled up, as if that could help protect him. I sat there, kind of stunned. I didn't expect John to just crack the guy in public without talking first or giving a warning push or shove.

I mean, I knew of John's reputation, but that was the first time I had ever seen him in action. He was everything his reputation said he was. John didn't ask for a second time for anything. If someone didn't immediately comply the first time, they were screwed.

But still, as tough as I was, it shocked the hell out of me to see him move so fast. It was as if someone pushed a button, or he flipped a switch, because within seconds, he had the guy down on the ground and half-knocked out.

Until now, all I'd ever known or witnessed about John when we were together was what an amazing and sweet guy he was, not only to me, but to everyone. He was always kind, humble, and acted like the perfect gentleman. When one would meet him, they would never know or think of him as being capable of the things he'd done.

Despite me being a little guy, I had status. I was considered to be living in high social standings. Because I had earned such a high level of respect, there were not many fights for me anymore. Don't get me wrong—if I had a problem, I'd definitely hit a switch and fight just like John did.

John and I were both respected and feared by the people around us. Interestingly, we each held slightly different philosophies as to how violence and fear brought us money. I was respected more for my social status in the hood, my bling, and the way I spoke to individuals who owed me. John Alite was more feared because he was outrageously aggressive and cutthroat. He believed in forced respect. His reputation was not to ask more than one time before he used violence.

I grew up and lived in one of the most violent cities in Eastern New York. My predominantly black neighborhood was a very dangerous place to be anytime of the day. The local precinct had too many murders to count, as people were getting killed on a daily basis. Not just anybody could walk through my neighborhood and expect not to have serious trouble.

But John could walk through my neighborhood all day long, and nobody would say shit to him because everybody knew John or knew of him. Even if they didn't know him, it was the way he looked and carried himself that would give anybody pause and think twice before messing with him. One could stereotype him easily by the clothes he'd wear, but for those who were street smart, they could see past his armor.

He looked, walked, and talked like a bonafide gangster. He just had this look about him, one that radiated confidence and power. He kept a cool and silent demeanor that could speak volumes. It was a look that said, "Don't fuck with me."

They don't make men like him anymore, and I'm talking about his toughness. They broke the mold when they made John.

I knew a lot of people in the music business. I've been to the Soul Train Music Awards. I've stayed at fancy hotels like the Peninsula Beverly Hills with singers like Kenny G, who had stayed two doors away from me. I had so much money, I could buy my way into anything, including the Grammys, the Oscars, the Golden Globes, or whatever else I wanted.

I had millions, and I loved showing off my money. I was one of those guys who was very flamboyant. I'd wear mink coats, Rolex watches, and drive Mercedes convertibles. I always wore big diamond earrings and rings on some of my fingers, and I'd have several thick gold chains around my neck. I loved my life of having power and prestige. I had made millions, and I had fun going through millions.

John Alite and I had gone to many big parties together. We'd hang out at parties hosted by Puff Daddy and Biggie Smalls and partied frequently together at the celebrity clubs.

There would be popular singers, actresses, models, producers, gangsters, and anyone who was anyone who had money. Those who were loaded could get the same type of priority access as someone who was famous.

Nails was another popular celebrity club on 14th Street in Manhattan. They didn't just let anyone in—you had to be known by somebody, but the bouncers knew John and I frequented there, and they knew we had money. The bouncers would stop the line outside the club when they saw us, and we'd bypass everyone.

I had ties to all of the black hip-hop groups. I loved music and was involved in the music industry. We knew all the rappers within our time era. Rappers like Tupac, Biggie, 50 Cent, Team McGriff, and many more.

John and I lived in a day and age where the rappers looked up to men like us because we were the true gangsters. It wasn't like we were sitting in a club, and then we'd go over to the rappers, acting exited like a groupie would. No, they'd see us in the club, and they were the ones coming over to our table to greet and talk to us. That's the type of status we had.

John always said rappers had the money and status, but they stayed with the gangsters because they wanted the attention. Most of the rappers were supposed to be real gangsters who rapped about violence, but the majority of those rappers hadn't been through shit. They were gangster wannabes. Instead, they sang about other people's lives. They wrote songs about real gangsters who put in the hard work and their stories.

Guys like me put in the hard work on the streets. Those rappers who hadn't been through shit witnessed first-hand what I had to do to get here. They were singing about men like me, Johnny, Supreme, Fat Cat, and my nephew Prince.

I had a lot of respect for Supreme. They lived the real gangster life, and they were successful rappers. Being both a gangster and a rapper proved to be a dangerous mix for the rapper Tupac, who was gunned down in Las Vegas, and whose murder has never been solved.

The Notorious B.I.G., or Biggie, as we called him, was considered to be one of the greatest rappers of all time. He was heavily involved in the East Coast-West Coast hip-hop feud. Eventually, he was murdered in a drive-by shooting in Los Angeles.

This was what the world of rap brings to the music industry and the streets. Violence and murders. Gangster-wannabe rappers are a fucked-up group of guys rapping words they don't understand. They could never understand or know their meaning because they didn't live the life.

Unlike most, I knew in my heart and soul that the life I was living would eventually have to come to an end. It was just a matter of time. The life itself was not as glamorous as everybody thought it was. I've witnessed time and time again that living this life has never really has ended well for anyone. It was only a matter of time before I figured I was either going to jail, going to die, or somebody in my family was going to get hurt over the things I did.

But sometimes, the money would come in so fast, I would get into a mindset that it was never going to stop. The money was never going stop. I was making millions and millions of dollars.

It wasn't so much the selling of drugs that destroyed so much of my life, it was me living in the streets the way I was. It was affecting my family in many ways. At one point, someone had broken into my house and tried to rob me. One of my neighbors had seen the robbers and called the police. Before the police arrived, the guys had already slipped out the back. The cops came in my home to get the details of what happened, and for whatever reason, they wound up searching my house.

My guess was the FBI was getting tips by some confidential informants, letting them know who I was. I could imagine how the conversation would go, "Oh, you got the guy TT. He's a big, big drug dealer." They didn't find drugs, but they found an AK-47 underneath my bed. I was arrested on the spot.

When it came to the gun charge, I didn't really give a shit about it. I was thinking that because I was super rich, I'd be out of jail within a few hours. A few hours wound up being several days. A day and a half in, I lost my patience. I was mad. I couldn't understand why the hell I was being held longer in jail when I was only facing a gun charge. The authorities kept making excuses and kept telling me not to worry about it.

The reason why I was still in jail was purposely kept a secret from me. I had been turned over to the FBI from the get-go. It took two full days in jail before me and my girlfriend were turned over into federal custody. Two men in suits and one lady came to my cell. One of them said, "Hey, TT, this is special agent so-and-so from the FBI." Another agent said, "This is the United States Marshall." By this time, I didn't even hear where the third agent was from.

I was in shock, and I remember saying to myself, "Like, wow. Oh my, God. I'm in some seriously deep shit."

I let them know right off that my girlfriend didn't have anything to do with my gun. It was my weapon, not hers. Thankfully, they decided to let her go.

I wound up staying behind bars almost for an entire week in federal custody. I was the only one in my family who had been to jail, and it was all because I was robbed in my own home.

I got out of jail the same day my bail was set. I was given a $750,000 bond. The second I got home, I moved us immediately. My girlfriend and I decided to stay near her mother's house, hoping to give her a little more sense of safety. However, the security of living closer to her family didn't last long.

The same guys who robbed me the first time tried to rob me again. I couldn't believe it. I was living in a brownstone, which was a high-class type of house to have. All I could think was, "Dude, does this look like a stash house I'm living in?" It was sarcastic anger, but I was really pissed off this time.

The robbers took a little bit of money that I kept in the house, but it didn't really amount to much. To me, it was nothing—maybe they took about $20,000 and a pair of diamond earrings. It was bullshit money for me.

I was living a glamorous life while I was living it, but the consequences behind the life was sobering. I was so blind to everything because of the money I was making. The problem was, I wasn't at home the day they robbed me, but my girlfriend was. They raped her. I couldn't express with words the amount of anger that was knotted up inside me. Someone I cared deeply about had been affected by all the street shit I did. I was having certain regrets, and things were starting to hit home.

My girlfriend was totally innocent in so many ways. She had no idea I was a major drug dealer. I deceived her when I first met her and thought I could get away with it. She thought my finances came from a rental car company I owned, renting out luxury cars. I didn't let her think any differently. I never showed her the part of my life that dealt with drugs.

One day, I was sitting in Lindenwood Diner in Brooklyn with a couple of guys having lunch. I was looking outside of the restaurant window when something caught my attention. "Wow," I said in a long drawl of disbelief. "Look, they're taking pictures of us," I said, pointing across eight lanes of traffic to the other side of the street.

"Oh shit," someone said, looking out the window. "Those guys are taking pictures of us," as if I hadn't just said that.

Being who I was at the time, a cocky young man, I had the attitude that I didn't give a rat's ass. No one was going to mess with me. I didn't care about the police, or anybody, because I knew I had enough money to pay my way out of anything.

I left the restaurant with my friends. Everyone piled into my red Porsche convertible, but not before I dropped the top. I opened my glove box where I kept a disposable camera and pulled it out to have on the ready. Then I cranked up my engine and took off.

I made the first U-turn I could, then drove back toward the diner, but on the opposite side of the road. I pulled alongside the car of the guys who were taking my picture. I boldly lifted my camera, pointing it at them, and then took their picture. We all laughed as my tires squealed and screeched as we sped off.

I think it was about four days later when I was sitting at a red light in my Porsche when all of a sudden, I hear, Whoop-Whoop! Then police sirens filled the air, coming at me from all angles. I was suddenly surrounded by cops. They came from every direction and out of nowhere.

"Holy shit," were the only words I could muster as I put the car in park and rolled down my window.

The same guys were with me from the Lindenwood Diner incident, and one of them seemed to know exactly what was going on. "TT—where's the camera? They want the pictures you took," he said in a panicked voice.

"It's in the glove compartment," I said.

The policeman approached and stopped at my window. He cut right to the chase. "You want to take pictures of the fucking FBI?" he asked in a voice that said he could make my life miserable.

Again, I was young and arrogant, and I said to the officer, "Hey—Y'all took my picture, so I took your picture."

He held out his hand for the camera.

"You'll see," the agent said, wearing an all-knowing smirk, taking the camera from my hand. "We'll see you later." He sounded so confident, self-assured, about seeing me later. His words only gave me a brief pause because nothing was stopping me from selling drugs. I was so good at living underground, I thought I was damn near untouchable.

It would be several months later, and I was on my way home when I noticed someone was following me. To be sure I wasn't being followed, I purposely ran a couple of stoplights. They ran every light I did.

When I turned down a one-way street, they would do the same. They were following me move for move.

Once I was finally able to lose them, I picked up my car phone and called my cousin who was living with me at the time. "Hey, listen up. I had a Jeep following me," I said. "I want you to get the gun and meet me outside with it." He stayed on the phone with me as he grabbed the gun. The moment he stepped out the front door, he stopped. "Yo," he said in shocked voice, "was it a white Jeep following you?"

"How'd you know?" I asked, taken off-guard.

"Well—they're parked in our driveway."

"Shit," I said under my breath. My cousin was a tough guy, and he wouldn't hesitate to shoot those guys in the Jeep. "Don't shoot the car!" I burst out. "Just don't shoot." I had to get him to back off, or we'd be fucked. "Can you see who's inside the car?"

"It's too dark, and their windows are tinted," he said.

"Go back inside and stay there," I ordered.

I slowly drove down my block until I could see them parked in front of my house. The second they spotted me, they backed out of the driveway. This was getting crazy. I quickly turned around to go the other way. The white Jeep jumped in behind me. Lucky for me, there was a precinct only three blocks from my house. I pulled up in front of the police station and got out of the car. I wasn't sure what was going to happen, but I stood there and waited for whatever to unfold.

The white Jeep didn't stop, but it drove by me really slowly. I could tell they were getting a good look at me as I stood there with my arms crossed. I was able to get their license plate number, so the next day, I gave the information to my lawyer. It was a matter of minutes before he came back with who the white Jeep belonged to. "Those mystery men in the white Jeep following you were the DEA."

I sat on the other side of the phone line, stunned. "What the hell was the DEA following me for?" I didn't expect this level of heat on me all of a sudden. It's like it came out of nowhere.

I had found out that when the government wanted someone, they would get them. Anyone who had the attention of the FBI, the DEA, or any other federal agency meant you were screwed. It wasn't a matter of if they'd get you, it was a matter of when.

The DEA had been tipped off somehow. They knew I was a major drug dealer, yet I had never been caught or arrested for drugs of any kind. I only had three convictions for firearms on my record. Having the DEA in my driveway was enough for me to realize they were never going to stop following or watching me until they had me in handcuffs and locked behind bars. It would be like living under a magnifying glass.

Two little sentences kept playing through my head. "You'll see," the agent had said, wearing an all-knowing smirk. "We'll see you later." That special agent who pulled me over would be known to have locked up about seven long-term guys I sold drugs to. The same guys I'd been to parties with were the same guys who got life. There were so many people I knew who got life in prison over drugs.

I've been to more funerals than guys have been to weddings or to graduations. I know more people serving life than I know who have graduated from high school.

That white Jeep full of DEAs made me understand I was eventually going to be another drug dealer sentenced to life. The proof was in the pudding. Not many people could recognize warning signs, and if they did, it still wouldn't be enough to stop them. I was at least thankful I could predict my ending, accept it, and get out before it was too late. I wasn't willing to give them my freedom or any more jail time.

The life I had been living was crazy, insane, and not normal. I'm astounded sometimes as to how I was able to get out of that life, not wind up in jail, or worse, get murdered. I got away from it all by the skin of my teeth. That just never happened in my world.

Most of those who were serving life who I had stayed in touch with were still rich. Every time I talked to them, they would tell me they would give up all their money just to have their freedom back. One really needs to think about that for a moment. Those men had acquired millions, yet it meant nothing without having their freedom. Those men would let it all go in the blink of an eye just to go back to the time they were free.

The crazy thing was, it didn't matter if one was a millionaire or not in jail. It wouldn't matter if they were a simple guy on the corner selling crack, a bank robber, or a big man on Wall Street doing Ponzi schemes. The most anyone could spend each month in the commissary was two hundred dollars, and those guys were millionaires! This made everyone in jail an equal in poverty.

The laws were a lot stricter when catching drug cases in the '80s as opposed to catching the same case in the 2020s. Jail sentences were harsh. As an example, let's say I had one gram of crack and someone else had ten grams of regular cocaine. At the time, the jail sentence was a hundred to one. That meant that if I got caught with one gram of crack, I could be charged with its equal, which would compute to me having been caught with a hundred grams of regular cocaine. That small amount of crack would have also meant a hundred times the trouble, had I been caught with it.

I have to say, the best president in my lifetime was Ronald Reagan. When Ronald Reagan won the office, it was like they opened the back door for drugs. The streets were flooded with drugs back then. In the year 2019 and beyond, the drugs have not been coming in like they used to. There are too many eyes on the street—terrorism, Homeland Security, drones, and so much other technology that makes it very difficult to sell drugs. No one could make the profits today that I was making back then. It's impossible.

If I could spread one message to our younger generation, it would be to tell them, "The street life is not a life worthy of living."

Ask any former drug dealer or any mobster. They would say the same thing, that time of making big money has come and gone. There is no money like that out there anymore. If they're lucky, they might make one or two thousand dollars at a time, but for what? To spend the rest of their life in prison?

I'm not on the street any longer, but I still have an ear to the ground. I know what's going on in the neighborhood. There's kids out there doing these bullshit maneuvers of small crime, and they're not even making any money doing them. It's not worth living that life.

Drugs will inevitably bring violence—whether it be through your hands or someone else's. One doesn't exist without the other. We were all held captive, swimming amongst each other like hungry sharks in an ocean of full of drugs and violence.

CHAPTER 16

John Alite - Mafia International

John Alite never wanted to be the average mobster; that wasn't him. He had a different outlook on the streets and how he fit into life. He had a very different perspective and made his own rules—rules that he never wavered from. He always believed in looking at everybody as an equal.

John didn't see that a person was white, Italian, Spanish, or black in order for him to respect them as a gangster or as a civilian. He looked at men as men, not as the color of their skin. The proof to this is that from a very young age, John had friends from all ethnic backgrounds, especially with the guys he grew up with in the streets. He simply just hit it off with the guys he thought were decent people.

Sixty percent of the students in Alite's elementary school were black during the time of racial tensions, but it never stopped him from associating and befriending them. Kevin Johnson was the first kid who, at five years old, was really good friends with John. Mike Williams had been captain of his baseball team when John was a freshman at Franklin J. Lane High School. John admired Mike and looked up to him before it was even chic to say, "A lot of my friends are black."

John explains how he feels about people and how he views street people:

I had a lot of respect for anyone who grew up on the streets with me. Guys like TT grew up to the left of my home in Brooklyn, and Supreme grew up on the streets in South Jamaica Queens.

I didn't believe one had to have an Italian background to be considered a real gangster—most of those real gangsters were weak anyway. Guys like Supreme, TT, and his associates in Brooklyn earned my respect of being full-fledged gangsters a long time ago. They were the real tough guys.

I was serving time at Loretto Prison in Pennsylvania when I stepped in to help a young Spanish kid. There were some cellmates trying to hurt him. The Sheriff in me came out, and I jumped right in to stop the fight. I had no idea who he was; I just helped the kid because he was young and outnumbered.

One of his cousins came to me and said, "Do you know who he is?"

I said, "No."

"Andre LaFlore." He told me the father was involved with the cartel. His mother divorced the father and was now very close to the president of Colombia.

Both parents had thanked me, telling me, "If you ever need anything from us, you let us know."

Later on, he would be in the newspaper, the article all about his mother and that she was going to visit her son in jail. Andre was a college kid who got arrested for money laundering. This had nothing to do with the father's cartel. The kid was doing something on his own with his friends and got caught.

Andre's family would be the very connection I would contact when I would go on the run to Colombia. The cartel helped me with immigration, passports, moving into a building that I rented for my hideout. The mother and their family members would bring me food and supplies. If I needed anything, they were always there taking care of me.

I started making connections through different members of the cartel who I met through them. I was moving drugs everywhere and doing business through mutual friends, interlocking everybody together, directly or indirectly. The network of friends and associates

I was acquiring never stopped growing. They came from all over the globe.

Even the friends and networks I made in prison reached beyond the prison walls.

I had a different belief than the Gottis. They were guys who wanted to keep others down, like a baby needing its mother's milk. They positioned their crew to make them struggle so they would always need them. I tried to treat my crew as good friends and take care of them. I was trying to make them all successful.

Johnny Burke was part of my crew, and when he was having problems, I'd always step up for him because he couldn't handle himself. He got shot and didn't even do anything. He was like the rest of my guys, never fighting back, and then asking me to always step in and take care of their problems both in and out of jail. I always did. He'd been shot, batted, and run over by a car right in front of his own wife in each occasion. Instead he came to me.

Johnny and I were scheduled to do a robbery together, but he was in the hospital. He had been run over by Brendan Gebert's car. He never would do anything about it or retaliate, but he would be directly involved with me in the conspiracy of Gebert's murder one day. When it came time to do work and kill him, though, he didn't want to be the shooter.

Since he couldn't do the robbery with me, I brought a young kid along with me, Dave D'Arpino. The plan was to invade a drug house in Suffolk County. The only gun we had, I handed over to Dave. The boy shit himself, too petrified to do the robbery.

After the robbery, I figured I made about four or five hundred thousand, cash. That amount of money for that type of robbery was huge in the early '80s. I definitely hit a jack pot.

I pulled out some of the cash and filled a small duffel bag full of green. I took the money to the hospital with me, then handed it over to Johnny.

He looked at me in confusion. "There's sixty four thousand in there," I told him, "Go buy your family a house, finally." He was always drunk and high and didn't ever do the right thing by his wife.

Once, I sent Johnny Burke to watch a drug dealer who was working for us, and instead of watching him, the guy went to jail. Then I found out Johnny had been skimming money from him while sleeping with the guy's wife.

One time, when Johnny Burke was in jail, he blackmailed us. He sent us messages through his mom that if we didn't give him money, he was going to start squealing about what he knew of our drug operations and the murder ring I was controlling. He was threatening all of us, and I was pissed. I knew we had to pay them off, but I would not forget this.

I made my guys go to his mom and give her twenty grand up front, and then all of us would make weekly payments to her to keep Burke quiet. Dave D'Arpino was the first to bitch and complain that he didn't want to give Burke any money. The funny thing was, when Dave started to cooperate in later years, he would blame everyone else, saying they talked first. Dave Patsy Adriano, Peter Sicara, Michael Malone, and me, we had all given him money for him to shut his mouth.

In much later years, Johnny would be serving time in the Citrus County Jail in Florida. At the same time, I was at Hillsborough County Jail, also in Florida, facing murder and RICO charges; most everyone was during this time. I was warned by the Dirty White Boys, an offshoot of a white supremacist gang that was at Citrus

County Jail with Johnny, that Johnny Burke had left the prison twice to meet with prosecutors.

Johnny had been transferred from New York to Citrus County to testify at a grand jury hearing against me. I knew it cost too much to send people from state to state to testify in a case, grand jury, or anything else unless they were going to talk. Also, if Johnny had let it be known beforehand that he was going to take the fifth, they never would have flown him from New York to speak before a grand jury hearing.

Johnny Burke and his lawyers were trying to cut deals with the prosecutor, and he left the prison twice on the days when no grand jury hearings were being held. The only reason why anyone would get to leave Citrus Jail was because they were going to rat.

The Dirty White Boys wanted to put their hands on Burke, but I said, "Hands off with Johnny, don't hurt him. Leave him alone." He was mine.

"We're putting him on the burn," one of the guys said. "He's buying everybody pizza but us."

"Why is he buying pizza?" I asked.

"Because he had problems with a couple of black guys in there, so he started paying them."

"Well, leave him alone, anyway," I told them. The gang might have quit talking to Johnny, but they didn't quit watching him. The Boys stole some paperwork Johnny had in his cell. They then brought it to me when we were in Hillsborough County Jail.

When guys were serving time in other jails around Florida, they had to come through Hillsborough Jail every time in order to go to court or hearings. Legal papers were the only thing anyone was allowed to have when leaving their jail, so the handoff was easy. Johnny had a long list of things he was going to talk about and people he was going to rat on.

A day or two went by, and I happened to see Johnny walking past my prison unit at Hillsborough. I had juice with the correctional officers, and I stopped one and said, "Get that guy over here and place him in sally port with me. I need to talk to him."

A sally port is a small, tight spot at the jail. I went through an automated, electric steel door and then waited until the next door to open up so I could get to the next section of the jail. It's like a hallway between sections with locked steel doors on both ends.

They opened the other door and let Johnny in the small tight section with me. We weren't cuffed, but we were in our prison uniforms. I grabbed his shirt and knotted the fabric in my fists, jerking his body forward.

"I know what you're doing here. You're going to testify against me at the grand jury," I growled in his face. "I already heard you left the prison twice, so I know you met with prosecutors." All he could do was stand there crying like a baby. "I knew you would send out that message through your mother, threatening you were going to talk unless we paid you." My grip tightened on his shirt, and I pushed his back against the wall. "At this point, Johnny, you're just another guy. Go and do what you've got to do because everybody else is fucking me anyway," my voice boomed. "So go ahead. Do what you want. I really don't give a fuck."

I released him with a shove, then banged on the door to be let out. I turned around and added, "Save yourself if you have to. I got my own things going on with Brazil, extradition law, and other things." I didn't try to stop him from testifying, and I didn't abuse him. I just walked away.

I found out later that Johnny had been giving information to his brother and his brother's wife, who was a city police officer. Friends and associates had been arrested because of Johnny. He was nothing but a double standard, a lowlife.

From what I had been told, Johnny had been giving information to his brother and wife for years. I also discovered that Johnny and his brother Tony had become best friends with an FBI agent who we all grew up with. They fixed up the agent's entire house. They did his floors, painted walls, and did other light construction, and they did it all for free.

It wasn't a wonder, then, when he got out on parole one time—and everyone said there was no way he could get parole with so many drug and other cases pending. Everybody had questioned him about that instance, which made us leerier of him than before.

The thing was, I never testified against Burke. I was asked to, but I wouldn't do it. I even fought like crazy with the prosecutor from the Eastern District of New York not to testify.

I held myself to a different kind of loyalty that I don't think ever really existed for others. Even when I did everything for my guys, it would never be enough to make them hold to the code. It was men like Johnny who had no honor. He was nothing more than a junkie, a coward, and weak-minded. Men like Johnny were the ones calling people rats while they were out meeting with the government at the same time.

CHAPTER 17

Gene Gotti in Jail / Joe Gambino

John Alite liked Gene Gotti on the streets, but not so much in jail. On the street, Gene had a successful shylock business with his long-time childhood friend, Joey Scopo, a friend who, in 1992, would meet a bad ending.

John understood why Gene was so frustrated, angry, and bitter in prison, and that likely ignited why he was serving bad time. It was hard enough on Gene Gotti that he was given a fifty-year bid instead of pleading out for nine years on his brother's orders, but Gene's angst went further back than this. Gene Gotti was straightened out before his brother John. When John became made, he pirated all of Gene's crew, naturally making him jealous, but losing his crew also made him look weak and ineffective. John Gotti's wife, Victoria, was the target of Gene's vitriol, possibly added to by his issues with his brother. Gene absolutely hated Victoria and passed around vicious innuendos and horrible stories about her. However, Gene would work with the kids in the neighborhood and was generous to ordinary people around him.

At the time Gene was in prison with John Alite, he was five foot ten and a healthy and strong man of fifty years with a receding hairline and a pot belly. Gene's big problem, as with many of the Gotti family, was his insecurity that pushed the envelope to paranoia.

The Federal Corrections Institution (FCI) McKean in Lewis Run, Pennsylvania, was a medium-security federal prison for male inmates. Alite was doing time in the same section of the prison as Joe Gambino. John respected Joe. He was a very low-key, quiet gentleman who kept mostly to himself. Joe Gambino didn't have an ego, and he stayed close-knit with a couple of inmates who were part of the Gambino crew. Joe believed in the life, as well as taking care of his extended family whether they were out in the streets or inside the prison walls. He would cook dinner, make coffee, and bake dessert for his friends every day, and he took pride in doing so.

As in most prisons, those of common ethnic descent stayed together in tight groups and didn't mingle with others outside of their factions. Even though Alite was Albanian, he would stay with the Italians because his affiliation was still with the Gambino crime family.

When I first got to the jail, Jimmy Calandra was Gene Gotti's cellmate. Gene wasn't the easiest man to live with. He went through a few cellmates, one of them being Jimmy Calandra from the Bath Avenue Boys. The Boys were a large and violent gang affiliated with the Bonanno Crime Family. Jimmy would eventually get straightened out and become a member of the Lucchese Family.

Jimmy couldn't stand living with Gene for very long, so he left. Gene begged me to be his cellmate because he didn't want somebody who was going to challenge his position within the cell. He figured since we knew each other, things would go smoothly if I stayed with him.

Gene wanted to feel like he was more important and more powerful, and because everybody knew the Gambino family name, he thought he deserved power and respect. Gene had the typical Gotti insecurities and had an inferiority complex, just like the rest of his family did.

When Gene wasn't getting the power and respect he thought was owed to him, he started mouthing off about Joe Gambino. I understood our laws—one of them being that we were not supposed to speak to anybody outside our own group. Gene had been breaking those rules and stepping on Joe's toes, constantly putting him down. He was telling other inmates from different groups that Joe was a drug-dealing, soft guy who amounted to nothing.

Gene found some guys from Detroit who listened to him. "Tank" was a big black man who held the power in that group. Gene told them Joe Gambino was just a cook and that he was just an underling because he was always serving us. Those men who were not affiliated with us didn't understand our way of life. They couldn't recognize the fact that Joe wasn't merely serving us, he was respecting the life and our laws within the Gambino family.

Joe didn't have to do anything for anyone, but that's how he chose to do his time, and he enjoyed giving himself to his so-called family. He did the things he did out of sincere friendship and the desire to keep the closeness of what we had on the street inside the jail.

Of course, Joe was unaware of the power play and deceit going on behind his back, but I wasn't. I could catch wind of almost anything because I was so diversified and integrated among all the groups and cultures. The men who were serving time with me were Patty Dellorusso, who held a high position in the Lucchese family; and Mikey Spinelli, who was a known killer and shooter for Anthony Gas Pipe. I was fairly certain Mikey had killed seven people thus far.

The three of us came together to personally speak to Gene Gotti about him running his mouth. We wanted to keep everything on the down low and take care of Gene ourselves, but our words of warning fell on deaf ears.

Gene inherently had a big mouth and would run it every chance he got; basically, he couldn't help it. He would sit and tell the entire table in our dining area about how bad his brother, John Gotti Senior, was on a daily basis. He'd also badmouth John's wife, usually referring to her as "Butch." He also ran his father's name through the mud, saying he was locked up for rape and that all he did was gamble and beat them up when they were kids.

Gene was constantly instigating problems, running down everyone he could, creating tensions and conflict among men both inside and outside of jail.

He was a miserable man because he was doing bad time, bitter because he could have served nine years, but John Gotti Senior wouldn't let him take the deal. He wound up getting fifty years instead, and is doing twenty-seven of them out of the fifty.

As if Gene had the power to drag his own brother down by telling everybody in jail, Senior's heroin money didn't go only into his own pocket, it went into his brother's pocket as well. This was no secret to any of us; everyone around us was moving heroin.

I happened to be out in the jail yard when a Spanish guy, Ramelle, came running up to me, panic evident in his eyes. Ramelle was a nice young kid from the Bronx who grew to be very close with Joe Gambino while in jail. Joe used to help him, and in turn, he would do some food errands for Joe, help him clean his cell, and do other miscellaneous things.

"What's wrong?" I asked him as he approached.

In a low and hurried voice, he said, "Gene and Joe are going at it in the unit. You better run back there and check it out. I think they're gonna fist fight." Our laws were that nobody could put their hands on a made guy, not even another made guy, or you'd get killed for it. That goes for on the street or inside prison. My guess was, word somehow got back to Joe about Gene badmouthing him.

I rushed back to the cell, and even before I could reach the unit, I could hear them yelling back and forth at each other. I got there in time to witness Gene pushing Joe and taking a swing at him. Joe ducked out of the way, getting grazed on the side of his head. Joe went right back into the fight, his fists flying. With me being thirty-five and in great shape from working out every day, I had no problem pushing them apart.

"Are you out of your fucking mind?" I yelled at Gene, my voice booming and echoing off the cell walls. "Are you out of your fucking mind doing this in front of all these inmates and talking about Joe like that? You think we don't know what you're doing?"

All of us exchanged a few more heated words. Gene knew not to raise a hand to me; he had no choice but to back down and leave. It would be this incident that would snowball into the next incident whereby things would start to get way out of hand.

Gene had decided to team up with Allie Calabrese. He was an Italian who was known to be a gangster's gangster. (The movie *The Irishman* mentioned him as violent gangster) He was also a bomb expert, prone to many cocaine binges, and was serving time in McKean like the rest of us. Allie had grown up around a guy named

Tommy who was a captain in the Cleveland mafia. Both Allie and Tommy were equally feared, except Tommy had the mannerisms of being a quiet gentleman, just like Joe Gambino. By Gene befriending Allie, it was an obvious power play on Gene's part. He was going to use Allie to be a strong arm for him, hoping to knock Joe down and acquire his own following.

Gene, Allie, and another guy teamed up against one of our men. His name was Danny. He was a kid out of the Bronx who stayed with Carmine "The Snake" Persico, the boss of the Colombo family. He also stayed with his brother Teddy Persico, who was currently serving time with us. The Persicos and Gottis didn't like each other, so Carmine and Teddy aligned with us on the streets. Teddy had slaughtered dozens of men during the Colombo wars in the early '90s.

Danny had told me Gene and Allie Calabrese had abused, threatened, and put their hands on him in the library. This made it the second time Gene had put his hands on a made man. He was out of control.

Gene was causing friction with everybody. He was harassing Charles "Chucky" Porter, who was the boss of the Pittsburgh Mafia, and Tony DeMaio, who was a strong arm for his crew. Chucky would later be known to be the highest-ranking member of La Cosa Nostra to turn on his own men, becoming an informant.

A few of the Boston crew members were not getting along with Gene, either. Billy McCarthy and Stevie Newell avoided him and hung out with us. There was a fine line between bravery and stupidity, and I knew what side of the line Gene was thinking from. He thought he was untouchable because of his name, but he would be wrong.

It was a cold and bitter night at McKean Prison. Everyone was wearing sweaters, hats, gloves, scarfs, and ski masks. It was the one time we could wear a ski mask over our faces and the guards wouldn't bother us. Joe Gambino would always walk the grounds every day, rain or shine, and the night's cold climate wouldn't be enough to give him pause.

Despite the fact that it was early evening, it was already dark outside from the thick clouds of misty snow.

"Johnny," Joe said, placing a hand on my shoulder. "I just had two guys put knives to my neck and stomach, threatening me. They told me I was going to have to pay them some astronomical figure, or they were going to stab me in the gut."

"Do you know who they are?" I asked with clenched teeth. My blood was boiling.

"They had their ski masks on," he said. "I didn't recognize their voices."

We wanted justice. All of us were infuriated, but we didn't know who they were. I had some very good connections in and out of jail. We were going to get to the bottom of this.

Gregory Heinz was the president of the Hell's Angels and a friend of mine. Everybody called him Pepe, but we called him Pepsi. I was able to get in touch with Pepsi, who would get a message out to the president of the Cleveland chapter. It was amazing to see all the creative methods and channels used by different groups as to how they'd send and receive messages both in and out of jail. I wanted help from my contacts to investigate who was messing with Joe Gambino and why.

Mark, the president of the Cleveland chapter of the Hells Angels, was able to visit me in jail to deliver the news in person. He told me it was Gene Gotti who was behind everything. He went to Allie Calabrese and told him Joe was loaded with money. He wanted Allie to set everything up with the black crew from Cleveland to step in and shake Joe Gambino down.

This was the second time Allie Calabrese got involved with trying to fuck with one of our guys. It was me and the same group of guys who talked to Gene the first time who were now talking to him again. We cornered him down in his cell, telling him we knew it was him who put the Cleveland crew on Joe.

The Cleveland crew didn't understand we couldn't let them get away with what they did. They had no right to cross over and get into our business. If we didn't take them back down a notch, they'd think the next mob guy to be put in jail would be free game.

A couple of days went by after our conversation with Gene. When some of the guys from the Cleveland crew came again for Joe and his money, I knew I was going to have to stop that fast.

Despite the divisions among us, it was still important to have mutual friends. Friendships in jail and the streets were key to making the right alliances. I made an effort to mingle with all of the groups.

Warren was a black man who was very powerful. He had control of the Cleveland crew and ran those streets like a king. We would play handball and work out together every day. We became really good friends.

When Warren heard the recent situation involved me, we held a meeting.

He immediately backed my side. He told his guys to lay down on this. Joe or the Gambinos weren't their business.

In the meantime, my guys and I didn't call anything off on Allie Calabrese; he wasn't part of the deal. We all knew Allie Calabrese was a diabetic. He'd go to the clinic every morning at the exact same time to get his shot of insulin.

It was me, Danny, a guy named Lee from Canada, and Antonio Parlavecchio who met up at the gym to make plans. Antonio Parlavecchio would be the one I would help in later years to bribe guards to help smuggle out vials of his sperm so his wife could get pregnant.

I was still having to live with Gene Gotti, who was still in tight with Allie. I had to be careful to stay on the down low and avoid suspicion. Like Allie, Gene had his own routine, too. He'd wake up every morning around six a.m. and go to the day room and sit. It was my habit to sleep in until nine a.m., so when I got up early one day, he raised a curious brow. I told him I couldn't sleep anymore and decided to take a walk.

Danny met me in the gym where we hid behind a doorway. Lee kept one of the guards busy in the upstairs recreation room. Antonio stood watch by the door. We had this timed perfectly, and just like clockwork, Allie was coming down the hall. As soon as he hit the doorway Danny and me tackled him, slamming him into the other side of the wall where the bathroom was.

Danny wanted his own revenge on Allie, and so he went at him hard. When most men would say to stop the fight and say enough was enough, we took it a step further because we were in a different zone of what raw and ruthless meant. Sometimes I couldn't discern if someone was either passed out or dead. It didn't matter to me; I wasn't going to stop anyway.

When we were decidedly finished beating the hell out of him, we dragged him inside the bathroom. We left him there sprawled out on the cold tile floor. We found out later that he was beaten so bad, he had to be taken to the local hospital. He never did come back to this jail. From what I understood through sources, that beating took a big toll on him. It stemmed into him having many other health complications.

Shortly after, he died.

BONUS CHAPTER

The Joey Scopo Hit

Entire books have been written about the Colombo crime family and the several wars the family lived through. The body count on the last war easily exceeded ten important men in just a two-year period among two factions of the treacherous Colombo family. Seemingly, like a throwback to the old days of Joe "The Boss" Masseria and Lucky Luciano, no one in power was safe.

From 1991—1993, the Colombo family was entrenched in a war that began in November of '91 and ended in October '93.

Joey Scopo was an acting boss under Vic Orena, who had been jailed for racketeering and murder. Orena was sentenced to three life sentences, plus 85 years.

On the other side was the infamous capo, chief enforcer, and hit-man, Greg Scarpa, A.K.A. "The Grim Reaper." He was at the top of the food chain after the Colombo crime boss, Carmine "The Snake" Persico, was imprisoned for racketeering in 1987 and got a hundred and thirty-nine years without parole. Scarpa wound up becoming an FBI informant. He died in prison from AIDS.

Orena, then Joey Scopo, was backed by John Gotti Senior to ultimately take over the Colombo family. It was common knowledge that Gotti was actually running the Orena faction of that family. Gotti had despised long-time Colombo boss John "The Snake" Persico, Jr., and the feeling was mutual.

John Alite had a keen, first-hand view of the internal feud going on for power in the Colombo crime family He explains the war in his own incomparable way.

Joey Scopo was best friends with Gene Gotti, who was Senior's younger brother. They enjoyed a shylock business with over a million dollars on the street.

That was a really big number in those years. Scopo and Gene even bought a house together so they could screw around on their wives and shit like that. I liked Joey a lot. He was a good guy and had a club down the street from our headquarters ,which was the Bergin Hunt and Fish Club on 101st Avenue in Ozone Park. His place was on 102nd or 103rd. Most Saturday nights, he would be at our club. He was a good guy and a good father to his son, Joe. In the life, Joey was well-liked, a good earner, and a handsome, strapping, six foot one tough guy, but a real gentleman. In fact, I remember when I got married at the Justice of the Peace, John Junior had signed as my witness. He was my best man, and Johnny Boy Ruggiano also was a witness. We then went to Altadonas with about fifteen people. Joey Scopo was there and gave a big envelope for that time. I forget, but it was a thousand to fifteen hundred.

Prior to the Scopo hit, Gotti Junior was the acting boss of the Gambino family, and Liborio "Barnie" Bellomo was acting boss of the Genovese family.

There was a sit-down at Anthony Amoroso's house on 85th Street and 162nd Avenue in Howard Beach to discuss messages from Senior to end the war. Barnie and Junior were there, and Mikey "Scars," Gotti Junior's captain, was there.

I had a bad argument with John Junior. I wanted to hit some guys in retaliation for our guys getting hit. Bobby Boriello had been murdered, and so were Eddie Leno and Anthony "Shorty" Mancuso, who was a made guy with the Gambinos. Shorty was killed at Bedrocks, a nightclub in Manhattan.

The club was owned by Steve Kaplan from the famous strip club The Gold Club in Atlanta. His girlfriend at the time was Rosanna Scotto of Channel 5 News. It was Kaplan's partner who killed Shorty, thinking Shorty was going to kill him. All these guys were killing without fear of retribution because they knew how weak and ineffective John Junior was.

I was supposed to hit Shorty's killer with Bobby Boriello on orders from Senior. We were to hit him near his apartment on the West Side and make it look like a robbery. Senior told us to lay on the guy. We laid on him three times. His building had no doorman, so it was a good place to whack him and rob him of his take from the nightclub. Suddenly, Senior called it off.

I laughed in Junior's face at the sit-down when he said they were going to end the war. There was no way that war was going to end at that point. A while later, Joey was hit outside his home.

Johnny Pappa had selected Anthony Russo, a captain, and Guerra, Curcio, and Sparacino as his crew to make the Scopo hit. Johnny and his hit crew robbed three cars and took them to Joey Scopo's house at 111th Street and 109th Avenue in Ozone Park. At about eleven at night, Joey showed up as the front passenger of a Nissan Altima, with his nephew driving. The crew boxed him in.

Sparacino shot into the car with a Mac 10, wounding the nephew in the shoulder and hitting Scopo in the stomach. Sparacino didn't finish the job, but instead took off running. Scopo got out of the car and saw Johnny Pappa hiding behind a tree. Pappa couldn't tell if Joey had a gun in his hand or if it was a cell phone. Joey threw the phone at Pappa, and in true tough-guy fashion, said, "You punk! What are you waiting for?" Pappa put four shots into Joey Scopo, with, I think the gun was a .380, killing him.

To tell you what a piece of garbage Pappa was, later on, he wound up killing two of his own crew members who were on the Scopo hit with him. Sparacino was killed because Pappa thought he was taking too much credit for the heat on the street.

Pappa was friends with one of his crew's brothers and was in his wedding party. When the detectives went to arrest Pappa at the church, he brandished his 9mm pistol. Bedlam ensued with the police chasing Pappa around the pews. He was arrested near the altar. The gun was found under a pew. He basically grew up with this particular family, yet had clipped the kid brother.

Johnny Pappa is serving four life-without-parole terms, plus forty years.

The Colombo war left bodies all over the streets.

In November 1991, Henry "Hank the Bank" Smurra, a Persico soldier, was gunned down in his car while going for coffee and donuts.

Tommy "Scars" Amato, a Genovese lieutenant, was killed on the street during a hit on Colombo associate Jerry Tolino in December of the same year.

A few days later, another Persico supporter, Rosario "Black Sam" Nastasi, was murdered inside his Belvedere Social Club in Brooklyn at the card table.

Right after that, an Orena soldier, Vincent "Vinnie Venus" Fusaro, was killed in front of his home in Bath Beach, Brooklyn, while hanging Christmas lights. So much for the mob not killing at the homes of their victims.

The next day at a bagel shop in Bay Ridge, Brooklyn, a civilian bystander, a teenager, was shot and killed during an attack on a Persico soldier.

The New Year, January 1992, saw Orena loyalist Nicholas "Nicky Black" Grancio shotgunned in his SUV in Brooklyn.

That March, Orena loyalists Johnny Minerva and Mike Imbergamo were slaughtered in a car at a Long Island diner.

Two months later, another Orena guy, Larry Lampisi, was splattered by a shotgun in front of his Brooklyn home.

Things were quiet for a few months, and then in October 1992, Steven "Lightning" Mancusi was murdered while getting into his car. Another Persico loyalist. They put Stevie Lightning's lights out that day.

Almost a year later, on October 20, 1993, Joey Scopo, the Capo and co-underboss, was killed in front of his house in Queens.

The war ended at the Scopo hit. The Persico faction kept the power in the Colombo Family.

CHAPTER 18

Gene Gotti in Jail / Joe Gambino

Gene was in a heated argument with Joe Gambino again. I was sick of him running his mouth and causing problems for all of us. I had enough. I decided it was time for me to intervene. Stepping in between the two men, I pushed Gene hard, slamming him into the cinder block wall of the cell. I wrapped my arm around his throat and squeezed, cutting off his air in a Jiu Jitsu style choke hold.

His dark brown eyes were wide with panic as I leaned in real close. "You're going to get a fucking beating from all of us if you don't stop running your big mouth," I threatened.

I squeezed his neck harder, then slapped him hard across the cheek. I could've hit Gene, but I was too mob-smart to do so. I choked him and slapped him around that day, but I didn't beat him up. I told everybody what I did was worse than getting a beating. It was more of an insult. I understood the life more than all of them.

The room fell silent behind me. I had just put my hands on a made man, but I didn't care. I think everyone was glad someone had the guts to finally step in to set Gene Gotti straight. I had crossed many lines both in and out of jail, consequences be damned, and this time was no different.

Warning after warning was given to Gene, and he was too hard-headed to listen. I was moving out of Gene's cell and into James Perry's. Gene was begging me to stay.

"Listen—you just don't fucking get it," I said, exasperated. I stopped packing my clothes and turned around to face Gene. "When I step out of this cell, you're going to see all the problems you have around this jail and in this fucking unit without me." He just kept trying to convince me to stay. "Forget it. That ain't never happening," I said as I walked out.

After the Cleveland incident, Gene was back at it, making new alliances. The next thing I knew, Gene got friendly with Tank, whose cell was next door to his. Tank was about six foot four, three hundred twenty pounds heavy, and an avid weightlifter from Detroit. He was just a strong jailhouse guy in shape. The mentality of the Gottis was that they always thought a weightlifter was their security. Tank knew what he was—a soft weightlifter, a drug dealer, and that's it. He wasn't a fucking rough-and-tough killer.

Another guy in the unit from Philly was a very close personal friend of mine, Butch. He was nicknamed Butch because he was big and brawny. He was about six foot even, and a real tough guy from Philadelphia. I had known him for a long time through our connections from the streets. His real name was Darryl Johnson. His mother was a schoolteacher, and I have to say, he came from a really good family, one I liked to stay in touch with.

The fact that prison was based on race and demographic and that he was black didn't have any bearing on our friendship. We were pretty tight-knit. It was considered taboo if one didn't stick to their own race in jail, but I didn't care. I used to sit on the other side of the chow hall and eat with him all the time. Nobody was going to say a word to me. Like Joe Gambino, Darryl liked to cook and showed respect for his crew by cooking for everyone.

I had discovered Gene had gone to Tank in secret, wanting to use him and his guys as leverage to abuse Joe. Gene was pushing new limits. Before anything could be done to Joe, I immediately went to Butch.

Butch was just as pissed off as I was. He was not the weightlifter that Tank was, but that didn't matter. He was tougher. Butch stepped up to Tank and yelled, "You get out of my fucking way. Mind your own fucking business, or I will beat you, stab you, any which way I want." Tank backed right out, washing his hands of the mafia business. Tank knew he was way out of his league.

Butch then threatened Gene, telling him to shut his mouth and stop all his posse schemes, or else. It was a known fact that if one went against Butch, they'd have a serious problem on their hands, and Gene knew it.

Gene knew he hit a brick wall, and it was our goal to put him in his place once and for all and to keep him there. Life was about to become very uncomfortable for him.

I put James Perry on Gene to roughen up and intimidate him. We were in our little common area when Perry picked up one of the plastic chairs and hurled it against Gene's back. James slapped him across the face as Gene stumbled forward. James towered over Gene, ordering him to get in the phone room to fight.

There was no way he was going to fight. He backed away, refusing to fight. James wasn't letting up; he was pushing Gene harder and harder, wanting the fight.

I yelled at James, "That's enough!" I just wanted James to abuse him, not beat him up. The puzzled look on James's face told me he couldn't understand why I was yelling at him to stop. He wasn't sure if I was serious or not. Then he decided I wasn't serious, because he slapped and pushed Gene again.

I got up, shoved the table aside to get to James. I pushed him into the phone room with such force that he fell to the floor. I was pissed. "I'll hurt you next time if you don't stop when I tell you to," I roared.

"Okay, man." He scrambled to his feet and backed up a couple steps. "I'll stop." Nothing would ever be done to James for abusing Gene and slapping him around. Years later, when John Gotti Junior was serving time in Ray Brook Prison, he ran into James Perry. He had asked James if he was the one who roughened up his uncle in jail. James said it was, and then the subject was dropped. Junior would do nothing to defend his family.

I was relentless in continually finding ways to ostracize Gene from every corner in the jail. I wanted to render him vulnerable and show him just how powerless he and his Gotti name was.

GQ would be the next man I'd use to harass Gene. GQ's real name was Louis Andino. He was a Latin King from Queens and a former acquaintance of mine.

"GQ," I whispered to the side. "Do me a favor."

"What's that?" he asked.

"I want you to go into Gene Gotti's cell. He has about sixty books of stamps in his locker," I told him. "I want you to take them out of his locker and keep them for yourself. They're yours."

GQ thought about it a moment, shrugged his shoulders, then said, "Sure, okay."

Of course, the moment Gene's books of stamps went missing, he was livid. He went on a rampage, talking big in front of inmates, wanting to find out who stole his stamps so he could seek revenge.

I nonchalantly walked over to where GQ was standing in the break room. "GQ, go tell him you took his stamps," I said with a sly grin. "Watch this punk. He's not going to do anything about it if you confront him."

GQ was small, but he was stocky and very strong. He walked over to Gene and said, "I took them, Gene. What are you going to do about it?" Gene pursed his lips and clenched his fists. He was frustrated because he knew he wasn't a tough guy, and he could do nothing but walk away with his tail between his legs.

I could get these guys to do whatever I wanted in a jail. How did I do it? It was simple. They knew I had the control in the jail. They knew I was nice to everybody. I was nice to my guys—always—in jail and on the streets. They knew they were good with me because they were secure with me. I would always do the right thing with them.

Shortly afterward, Gene approached me outside in the fenced yard.

"Can I talk to you?" he asked.

"Sure," I said. "Let's take a walk."

As we walked along the fence line, he started talking. "Everybody in this jail knows it was you guys who beat up Allie Calabrese." He stopped for a moment and looked me in the eyes. "He was my best friend."

"You know, Gene, you're supposed to be a made member of the Gambino family and a captain. There's no reason I should have to discuss this in jail or anywhere else with you." This was all his fault. He was the one who'd decided to bring Allie into our personal affairs. "How dare you go behind everyone and try to shake down one of our very own guys…and how dare you embarrass our Borgata."

He looked off into the distance, asking, "What do I do? How do I walk around here now?" His voice was lone and distant. He had reached the end of his rope and was worn down. He should be embarrassed for himself, but I'm not sure he was capable of self-reflection.

"This is how you walk around, Gene," I informed him coldly and callously. "From now on, you shut your fucking mouth and don't ever go near Joe Gambino again."

He nodded his head, acknowledging the demands. "When anybody asks you what happened to Allie Calabrese, you tell them you had it done. That should settle your situation in here," I said, extending him a little undeserved mercy.

I stepped over to my friend Mark Giuliani to have a few words. Mark was a Wall Street guy from Cherry Hill. He was in really good shape, and I knew he wouldn't hesitate to do me a favor.

"Hey. I want you to step over to Gene right now and tell him you have a problem with him. Tell him you want to fight him."

"No problem," he said. He brushed by me and went over to where Gene was standing and told him exactly what I said to say. Mark squared off his shoulders as if he actually did have a problem and was willing to fight. Mark then told Gene to go into the gym's bathroom. Gene held up his hands in a surrender.

We had driven our point home. Everybody now understood Gene was nothing but idle talk and didn't control anything like he had everybody believing.

Our own inner circle would have very little or nothing to do with Gene. Everywhere he went, he'd find himself being an outcast for years to come. Later, when all of us had transferred out of McKean, we never saw Gene again, but of course, we never talked to him either.

Gene was a walking disaster, a train wreck waiting to happen, as he kept demoralizing the very structure and foundation of our secret society. We were beginning to stand for a brotherhood and an organization that was falling apart at the seams.

It was the Gambino family who I respected the most. They were civil, quiet, and low-key gentlemen who lived by the code, dedicated themselves to the life, maintained and held fast to its rules. Whether or not anybody agreed with the lifestyle, at least in my eyes, they deserved respect for the way they handled themselves, their family, and their businesses.

Despite any decent qualities one could find in any faction, everyone's life still hung by a very fine thread. Living in and among the mob wasn't a cake walk. It was full of treachery, deception, backstabbing, and explosive violence. Living in the life of the mafia was like walking in an active minefield, never knowing if one's next step would mean their death.

CHAPTER 19

Frankie Gets Murdered

Flashing back to a time before Alite did his bid at FCI McKean, more treachery among friends was about to take place. John was doing something that was rare in his lifestyle. He was actually relaxing at his estate in Cherry Hill, New Jersey, for a few days. The moment of respite, however, was shattered by terrible and unexpected news. It was about Frankie Burke.

I glanced at the clock and cursed. It was three in the morning. Lucky and King, my Rottweiler and Husky, were barking their heads off. Awake now, I heard loud knocking and banging on the front door over the barking of the dogs. Then the doorbell rang, followed by more pounding. It was non-fucking-stop, which told me something was very wrong.

I half-stumbled around, trying to wake up. I put on my bathrobe, then grabbed the pistol from my nightstand. As I headed to the front door, I hid the gun inside my robe. I turned on the hall light. "Back off, Lucky and King," I said gruffly, trying to step around them.

I opened the front door and asked, "What the fuck is going on?" A few guys from my crew were standing at my door, and by the look in their eyes, I could tell something bad happened. It was Big Dom, Fat Larry, and his brothers Frankie and Joey. They were all acting nervous, but I could sense a level of fear.

Larry shifted on his feet as if he were trying to find the right words.

"What the fuck, man?" I snapped impatiently.

"Vito just shot Frankie," Joey blurted out.

"What!?" I stood stunned for a quick second as Joey told me the story.

"He shot Frankie in the head five times." I couldn't believe what I was hearing; we were all friends.

"We were at the Black Gate. We were just partying and getting high and chasing girls, just like any other night." The Black Gate was an after-hours club and one of our main hangouts. Everybody would go to this bar late at night to keep getting drunk and high. The downstairs was the bar area and a pool room, but I believe it was the upstairs where men could pay for prostitutes.

They'd party a lot, but no one was really a cocaine junkie. We had been dealing in drugs together for years. I was their supplier, and they, in turn, would supply to each other.

"Frankie sold Tito cut coke. They got into a really bad argument about him stepping on it too much," Larry said. Tito would know if it was cut; from what I understood, he was smoking coke, so he knew what a quality product was.

"Tito and Frankie took the argument outside. I thought they'd have their little fight and get over it. We followed them out, but by that time, Tito had pulled a gun from his car. It happened so quick. He shot Frankie point blank in the head, and as he was going down, he unloaded four more shots on him."

The main thing running through my mind in that moment was how the hell I was going to show up at the Burke's house and tell his mother and sisters that Frankie was dead. "Son of a bitch," I muttered.

Frankie mother's name was Mickey. She was a woman I highly respected and genuinely liked. She was strong, intelligent, and had great sense of humor like Frankie. She was a great mother to all her kids and always good to me. I was fortunate to have been friendly with their family.

The fact that my guys were there and didn't do anything to help stop the shooting in the first place was not a good thing for them. They could be held fully responsible for Frankie's death for watching things get out of hand and then not stepping in. They wound up begging me not to give up their names and to help them to cover it up.

"Why the fuck didn't any of you stop it?" I yelled.

"It all happened so fast," Big Tom explained. "We thought he just stormed out, and when he came back in the bar, his gun was already cocked and pointed at Frankie."

"They were both very high," Joey added.

I was pissed off and disgusted that no one was able to read into the situation for what it was and then be proactive. Now I was going to have to find a way to keep their names out of it because they weren't safe. I'd have to prep them with a solid alibi.

I threw on a pair of jeans and a t-shirt. I was going to the Black Gate to see for myself. No one wanted to ride with me because I was in a mode to explode. My adrenaline was running high. I was just as pissed off at my guys as I was at Tito.

I tucked my gun away, then headed out the door. I drove into Brooklyn to the Black Gate. When I got there, the police were swarming the entire block, their flashing blue-and-white lights lighting up the entire street. I hung back out of the crowd of people. I could see in the distance that the all-too-familiar yellow crime scene tape already roped off on the sidewalk, and in the middle of the yellow tape was my good friend laying lifeless under a police cover—dead.

Most of the policemen wrote notes in their pad as they interviewed witnesses. The word was already out on the street that Tito Ortiz did the shooting and had been arrested. Tito was our friend who owned the Black Gate bar. The guys on the street and the mobsters—we all knew who the killer really was.

The authorities had arrested the wrong man. Part of the problem was that Vito went by Tito on the street and looked similar to the Tito who owned the bar. While Tito Ortiz was in jail, he wound up making bail because the police had no weapon to prove him guilty.

They had nothing physical. The other problem the investigators were having was that they had no proof on Tito, and no one was coming forward to turn in Vito.

I put my car back in gear and then headed in the direction of the Burkes's home. The entire drive, I was thinking about how I was going to tell them the news. I knew there was never going to be a good way to find the right words at a time like this.

I was upset about Frankie; he was a really good friend. I was going to miss him, but the reality was, death surrounded me every day. I was too battle-hardened to get overly emotional.

My mind flipped back to the time Frankie and I killed two guys together. It was about six months before, over a drug debt that was owed to his dad, Jimmy Burke. We shot them not too far from where the Black Gate was. With Frankie gone now, no one would ever be able to hold those murders over my head. I'd be a liar if I didn't admit to some level of relief that I couldn't get charged for that double murder any longer. Now there would be no witnesses, and no one would be able to squeal on me. I don't have to think about it ever again.

Frankie liked living the life. It wasn't about the money for him. His father was a famous gangster who helped raise him. He always wanted to be with and do whatever his father did. He didn't want to be a spoiled rich kid. He wanted to be a tough guy, follow in his father's footsteps, and live up to his dad's reputation.

Frankie was a lot like his father—both really nice guys who liked to play and joke around a lot. I remember Frankie coming to my house one night about two in the morning driving a fire engine truck. He barreled into the complex with the sirens on full blast, waking up the entire building. He was yelling that there was a fire. Everybody was running out of the building, screaming, and freaking out. I found myself grinning at what he had done next. Frankie had come strolling through my front door, drunk, and with a handful of girls.

My mind had wandered so much, I found myself not really remembering the last two turns. I pulled into Frankie's driveway and parked.

I was surrounded by the quiet in the night's air like a dark rain cloud about to let loose. I got out of my car and went to knock on their front door just hours before dawn. A few harder knocks on the door finally roused them from sleep.

It was Kathy, Frankie's sister, who opened the door. She knew something had happened but was speechless. We both stood there for a moment, staring at each other, her eyes full of questions, yet her heart not wanting to know the answers.

"Kathy," I said solemnly, "I don't even know…" I paused, tripping over my words, trying to find the right thing to say, but couldn't. "I just got to tell it to you straight—Frankie's dead."

With a loud gasp, the palm of her hand covered her mouth as she stood there in shock. "He got shot five or six times in the head in Brooklyn," I told her. There's just no sugarcoating this kind of news. She didn't really freak out in that moment, but she started to shake like crazy, so I reached out for her. She burst into an uncontrollable sob. The look of pain in her eyes was something that would be etched in my memory forever. I took the initiative and guided her into the house. The both of us knew I would have to be the one to tell Mrs. Burke.

She was already awake now, standing at the bottom of the stairs in her bathrobe. She glanced at her daughter and saw her tears. She held out her hand toward the living room, offering me the silent gesture for us to join her there. As I passed by Kathy, she grabbed my arm and held on for support as we headed toward the living room.

Kathy sunk into the sofa, burying her face in her hands. Her shoulders shook as she silently cried. Then Robin, Frankie's other sister, came into the living room and sat beside her mother to see what was going on. Frankie's younger brother, Larry, was too young to understand.

By the time I was done explaining what I knew, the police had called the Burke house. It had been decided that Kathy should be the family member to go to Kings County Hospital in Brooklyn to identify her brother's body. She was in no shape to drive. I didn't even give the family an option. I was taking her there myself.

Frankie and his family had always been close to me. I had this huge brick in my gut, not only for the family's pain, but for the fact that I knew who shot Frankie. I wasn't not saying much of anything or accusing anybody at this point, as some of it was still hearsay. I was holding my cards close to my chest because I first had to find out if it was truly Vito. I also knew it was a guaranteed death sentence to whomever it was who killed Frankie.

I drove Kathy to Kings County Hospital. She had cried the entire way, leaving her eyes bloodshot by the time we got to the hospital.

She held onto to me for support as we made our way to the morgue. As nice as it would be for Kathy not to have to see her brother in this condition, she still had to identify the body.

We walked in the room as a police officer was unzipping the large, black body bag. Frankie's head was all shot up with bullet holes; his face was a bloody mess. Without a doubt, Kathy would remember this moment for her lifetime. It was tragic that this would be Kathy's final memory of what her brother looked like and not a memory of before his murder.

Once the technical shit was out of the way, we left. I drove her all the way home in silence. I wound up staying with the family for quite some time. I stayed because I felt my presence was me paying my respects and giving them support. We discussed how we were going to tell Jimmy that his son was just murdered. My heart hurt for this family.

I was already on parole for a gun charge, taking a gun that wasn't mine. I copped a plea on it. If I was seen here at their house and cops were stopping by to ask questions, they'd find out right away I was breaking my parole. I knew the Burkes would never turn me in, but anybody else who stopped by to pay their respects, such as another wise guy, could make one phone call and turn me in. I knew people were going to start showing up throughout the day, so I needed to leave before anyone came by.

Vito Scaglione owned Father and Son's, a hair cutting salon that was just a few doors down from the P.M. Pub, our regular hangout. His barbershop was a place most gangsters frequented for a haircut and shave. I had to tell Tito he was not allowed in our bar anymore because of what he did. He wound up getting black-balled by everybody.

Over the next couple of days, we laid low and told everyone to mind their own business, keep their mouth shut, and not to talk to anybody. Tensions were high. It was a possibility I could be given the order to hit Vito. Even though he was one of our friends, we all knew what the life was. It was a merciless system that held no second chances.

The order could come from either the Lucchese family or the Bonanno family. Frankie's father could tell the Bonanno family that they had to kill one of their guys for killing his son, or he could have the family kill Vito himself. There were so many different ways this could go down.

Vito's brother-in-law, Dominic Cataldo, was a wise guy who was with the Colombo crew. I had no doubt that Dominic would be on the carpet to set up the hit on his brother-in-law.

The length of time that passed by after someone was marked for murder varied from days to months. Sometimes the time lapse was done on purpose in order to give their victim a false sense of security. This was called rocking them to sleep. But those who knew how the mafia worked knew the mafia never forgot.

Occasionally, there would be a delay on striking back because calling for a hit on another made man sometimes took time, and quite often, the crime families argued back and forth about what was to be done—then how to proceed with the how and when.

Vito knew he was getting killed. He could've taken it on the hop and ran. He could've gone to try and hide in Italy. He could've done a lot of things to get away, but he chose not to. I guess maybe he realized he was high the night he shot Frankie and convinced himself he knew he deserved to die for what he did.

Everyone knew Vito took a nap in his barbershop chair every day. He would recline his old-style barbershop chair with his back facing the door. He'd lay his head back as if he were going to get a shave, then close his eyes to sleep. Guys would always be walking in and out, but Vito never flinched as people came and went.

Four months later, when he was sitting in his chair watching T.V., three men went into his barbershop and shot him ten times in the back of the head. The ten bullets signified double the retribution for the number of bullets he used on Frankie.

For the hundredth time, I told myself that this was the very life I'd been wanting to live. Even through all of the death, pain, and loss, I still believed I was exactly where I wanted and needed to be.

CHAPTER 20

Terrorists in Jail

For many years, my home would be the Metropolitan Correctional Center in New York, and it was referred to as MCC for short. It was a United States federal high-rise dungeon of a jail located in Manhattan's financial district. It was a filthy and dilapidated building full of vermin, infestation, and overflowing sewage. I was living in inhumane living conditions. MCC was an absolute hell hole, and the goal was just to try and stay alive without losing one's mind.

MCC could be compared with that of the jails in other foreign countries. One thing that surprised me at this American facility was the number of Muslims behind bars who were facing terrorism charges. There were plenty of ex-terrorists in the unit, many being high-ranking al-Qaeda operatives. The outside world had no clue the government had all these terrorists hidden inside the walls of MCC. There were other famous, high-profile prisoners who were concealed here as well.

Of note, the son of Cathy Zeta-Jones and Mike Douglas, John Gotti, Jackie D'Amico, Bernard Madoff, terrorists Ramzi Yousef and Omar Abdel Rahman, and the sex offender Jeffrey Epstein, to name a few.

I understood the need to keep the existence of al-Qaeda on the down low from the public because I had no doubt there would be an uproar on the streets had most Americans known where these bastards were kept. American men and women alike would want their heads, and I was no different.

Those men were at a severe disadvantage on our soil. They had zero power within our jail system, and I took full advantage of it. I despised those men like nothing else. I would abuse them any way I could, as often as I could, and took advantage of every window of opportunity to mess with them when the guards weren't looking.

One terrorist I hated the most was Mohammed Babar. He worked behind the scenes, a radical who served al-Qaeda and participated in the organization of large-scale plots against the United States and other countries.

Mohammed Junaid Babar was born in Pakistan in 1977 and moved with his family to Queens, New York, as a very young boy. He attended military school on Long Island and later became a radical following the Sunni Islam views while attending St. John's University. In the summer of 2003, he helped to set up a terrorist training camp. He faced 70 years in prison. Babar cooperated with federal U.S. authorities and testified in March 2006 against other terrorists accused of plotting the July 2005 London bombings blowing up three trains and a double-decker bus. He was released for time served, which was highly criticized by the British government. Ironically, Babar's mother survived the September 11, 2001, suicide bombing of the World Trade Center. She worked on the 9th floor of building.

Mohammad was responsible for killing and injuring a mass of innocent people, and I wanted to see him hang. He was an odd character who was obsessive-compulsive with germs. He didn't want to shake anyone's hand, and I certainly wouldn't shake his hand if I were paid. If somebody shook his hand, he would go running to wash his hands ten times over in the sink. I found amusement in watching him freak out like a little girl when he came into contact with others, and then I harassed him about it. I harassed him about a lot of things.

"I want to understand," I said in ridicule. "You're a fucking terrorist, but you like the New York Mets?" Mohammad was a huge fan of the American baseball team the Mets. "Do you have the New York Mets playing in Afghanistan?" I mocked.

"No," he said, knowing he was in a losing game of Q & A with me. Mohammad would always keep his answers as short as possible to avoid the conflict and a sarcasm he couldn't compete with. He was from Jamaica Avenue in Richmond Hill, and he went to Richmond Hill High School, which was a neighborhood located adjacent to mine.

"Well, you went to high school in Richmond Hill, but you were born in Afghanistan. I don't understand—if you're so anti-U.S., why are you so pro-U.S. in the things that you like?" I didn't care about him or his petty answers. I just wanted to play mind games with him. "You are full of double standards," I said harshly. "You like all the freedoms and diverse culture our country has to offer, but yet, you hate America."

I would let his mind get in a twist, and then I would bounce from one subject to the other, bombarding him with quick wit and making him stumble over his words.

"Let me ask you this. Would you have your own son wear a bomb?" I asked him, being sarcastic, yet curious of his answer.

"Yeah," he replied.

"Wow," I said, not wanting to believe someone could actually sacrifice their own flesh and blood, an innocent child. "You mean you would actually have your own son wear a bomb?" I asked incredulously.

"Yes, I would," he said, looking back at me with his beady, dark eyes. I wanted to kill that terrorist right where he stood.

"Well, if you like Afghanistan so much, why did you stay here in the United States for so long?" I asked contemptuously.

"Why do you keep fucking with me?" he asked, exhausted, tired of me bombarding him with questions he had no answers for. We'd always go round and round like this, and when he got to his wit's end, he'd always ask the same question: "Why do you keep fucking with me?"

My answer would always the same. "Because I can't stand you," I'd hiss, full of hatred. "You're a fucking terrorist. You blew up fucking trains in London. You killed people like a fucking coward."

Then I knocked him down another peg, "You don't have the balls to go do the missions yourself. You're a powerless piece of shit."

I was waiting for him to give me any excuse possible to smack him around, but he pursed his lips and stayed silent. I'd kept egging him on, "You're such a screw up, I don't think you can even do ten push-ups right."

This guy used to do a lot of push-ups, actually, but I wanted to harass him any way I could. I stepped up to him, then added, "You know what the problem is with guys like you? You don't do anything good—you can't even do a push-up good."

I left him with that, but we both knew it wasn't the end. I'd be back the next day, or the day after, and then start the process all over again, just to mentally mess with him.

Bryant Vinas was a terrorist from Long Island who participated in two al-Qaeda rocket attacks on U.S. soldiers in Afghanistan. He was convicted for participating in and supporting many al-Qaeda plots in Afghanistan against the U.S. He was captured by Pakistani forces and then transferred into FBI custody, where he would then plead guilty to the charges against him.

What was really bizarre to me was that Bryant was a fan of mine. He knew exactly who I was, and he used to talk about me all the time to his friends. "Why the fuck do you keep following me around? I don't like you," I'd stop and turn around, asking in frustration. It was not in his best interest to follow me around in jail like a puppy dog; I couldn't stand him.

"You don't understand," he'd say in his Taliban accent, pleading for me to understand. "You don't understand."

No matter what I'd say or how bad I abused him, he still tried to hang around me. "You're not really Muslim," I would sometimes say, taunting him. "I don't know what the fuck you're pretending to be, but you're not Muslim."

"Yes, I am," he'd reply, defending his religion.

I didn't have respect for men like him because they weren't really studying the Quran. "You have hijacked sacred and moral practices. You distort your religion because you're self-serving. You live to hate."

"How would you know what the Quran says?" he challenged.

I had respect for the Muslim religion. In fact, I was from a Muslim family. I stepped forward and pointed my finger into his small chest, driving my point home. "I'm Albanian. I was raised by a Muslim family. My grandfather's birth name was Ali, my grandmother was Fatima, and my father was Mohammed. I know more about the religion than you do.

"Real Muslims are just religious, good, peaceful, and loving people, not sick fanaticals like you." People were always relating Muslims to these idiot, nut terrorists, giving the religion a bad name.

Even though I had long ago converted my faith over to Christianity, everything I told him was true. He was hurting his own religion by succumbing to fanaticism. He didn't have a brain of his own to think for himself.

"I'm not that fake piece-of-shit you and all your radical fanatics are," I told him. "You don't even know what you're doing when you pray to your God in jail."

I despised the fact that they were given the right to gather in their little groups and pray in their twisted, terrorist ways as they still plotted against us.

I used to walk by their little room when they were praying toward Mecca and stick my head in, cursing a string of obscenities while they were praying. I did everything I could to disrupt their prayer time. Everybody would get mad at me for it, but I didn't care. They would tell me how disrespectful I was being, but my response was always the same to them. They'd never get respect from me—never.

I was relentless in my mission, wanting to make their daily lives as miserable as possible. I even used to throw human shit in their beds, and I detested other guys who were Americans who would get friendly with them.

It was a habit of mine to go by the terrorists' cells as often as possible. Any chance I got, I paid them a visit with the sole intent of abusing them in any way I could. I was aggressively verbal, degrading them, trying to get them to react so they'd fight me, but they were cowards to the core.

A couple days later, I visited Bryant's cell. I was messing with his mind in a way that had his eyes welling up with tears.

"You don't know how much I want to kill myself," he said despairingly. "You just don't know."

I raised a brow in question. "Why would you want to kill yourself?" I asked, not giving a fuck about his answer. "You've got all these angels and seventy-something virgin maidens awaiting you in paradise," I mocked. "Don't you get like nine lives too?" I kept taunting him with all the things he'd supposedly get once he died.

"Tell me something," I said, full of sarcasm, "I just want to understand something—you mean to tell me you dressed up like a girl to get into the Taliban, just so you could shoot rockets at the United States soldiers?"

"It didn't go off," he argued.

I replied, "The fact that you shot a rocket at U.S. troops and because it didn't go off makes everything okay? Why the fuck would anyone trust that the rockets never went off, just because you said that to be true?" It was all bullshit, and I wouldn't be surprised if he had killed and shot dozens of our men in the past year.

"I just want to kill myself," he said, breaking out into a cry. He was having a weak moment, a pity-party.

When he said he wanted to kill himself, I offered again to lend him a helping hand. "Well, come on then," I taunted. "Let me help you."

He then thought he had a moment of strength, staring at me in defiance. "You think I wouldn't hang myself?" he asked, as if he were brave enough to take his own life. "You think I wouldn't hang myself?"

"Bryant, I just told you—I'll help you," I said sarcastically, as if I were some angel in light. I shifted my gaze to the ceiling as I pointed upward. "Look," I said, showing him. "We can get you boosted up there." I looked back to Bryant, repeating, "I'll help you kill yourself, right now."

We went back and forth for a while longer, then he got a little slick with his mouth. I got in his face within seconds, and then wrapped my fingers around his scrawny neck, chocking off his airway.

"Listen, Vinas, or Bryant, or whatever the fuck your name is," I said, having lost my temper. "You're just a little pussy kid with a conflicted sense of identity who's been brainwashed, and you're too stupid to realize it. You don't even have what it takes to survive in this jail. You're a weak-minded sadistic parasite who murders innocent people," I growled.

He was desperate for air, going crazy, flailing around, and trying to break free. I used every bit of my strength to hold him in place while I strangulated him. I leaned in close, smelling the putrid smell of his body odor. I whispered in a calm, reassuring tone of mockery, one that belied my hatred, "What's the matter? Why are you fighting me?" Panic stricken, his fingers dug into mine, trying to pry them off him. "You wanted to die, right?" I bit out between clenched teeth. "So I'm fucking doing it for you now."

While I was choking him to death, one of the inmates across from us discovered what was going on. He was a bald guy named Dino, a drug dealer from Colombia, and he squealed to the guards. The enforcements came quickly, pulling me off him with much effort on their part. I wasn't about to give up so easily. I had him choked out, and I knew that with just a little bit longer, I would've had him.

We both wound up in solitary confinement in one of the wings upstairs. I wasn't charged with attempted murder. I was charged with assault—a fight that warranted an investigation. Obviously, I stated I wasn't trying to kill him to avoid the possibility of a more serious charge.

Solitary confinement was brutal enough to deal with all by itself. We didn't need the guards doling out barbarous acts for their own sadistic pleasure on top of living in inhumane conditions. All of us high-profile inmates understood that we deserved what we got. All of us contended with solitary confinement, fights, and acts of violence every day. It just came with the territory.

One would think the United States prison system would be held to a higher standard of living and made to practice sanitary conditions. Moreover, to hold the guards to a level of integrity, practicing professionalism in their job, but they were not held accountable. The problem was, the public living in the outside world didn't understand the level of contamination and evil we waded through day-in and day-out.

I'm just like any other guy in jail—I'm a human being, and there were times in jail that I struggled. The jail time itself wasn't the hardest part for me, it's just something I became used to. Other men might've struggled behind bars, but that's not what made me break down. The suffering points in jail that most don't understand is that we can't be there when a close relative passes away. We worry about our family and our children's safety, and we wonder if they have been cast out on the street because they couldn't make ends meet. The mental anguish was overwhelming at times.

The way most of us dealt with stress was to not deal with it directly. In order to get our minds off what was really bothering us, we'd exchange it for something we felt we had some control over. Sometimes we'd concentrate on being sick and made excuses to see the doctor. Having hours on end in confinement, we'd have to use our imagination to focus on anything and everything to avoid facing the truth. But sometimes it wasn't enough; sometimes, our demons surfaced and taunted us.

Claudia, my wife, had cancer, and I was scared she was going to die, and I couldn't be there for her. At the same time, I was crying in solitary confinement over this situation when one of the guards had walked by and stopped to purposely provoke me. He mocked me as if I were a weakling and crying like a baby because I was stuck in a jail cell.

The anger that flowed through my body in that moment made me feel I could rip those bars apart like Superman and beat the guard shitless, taking him to his last breath. I stopped crying immediately, and my voice roared with contempt, reverberating off my cell walls, "Motherfucker, you open that gate, and we will see how scared I am about being here. Because I will fucking kill you." I wasn't kidding. I meant every word because he had me so hyped up with anger. I really wanted to get my hands on him. It wasn't that all the guards were bad, but they all weren't good, either.

Legally, the guards have to give the inmates three showers a week, but they'd wait until three or four o'clock in the morning to turn them on. Being in a high-security cell, the shower was in the cell with me, so they didn't have to move me. They'd bang on your door and yell at you to get in the shower. The odd hours were purposely picked because they wanted to fuck with us mentally. Secondly, it was wintertime, and the room was already ice-cold, and so was the water. All of us were freezing, as we were only issued a thin sheet to keep warm, but if you didn't get in the ice-cold shower, you didn't wash—it was that simple.

We had no choice but to get up and go wash. We'd run into the glacial water, spending seconds trying to clean up, and then run the hell out with teeth chattering and our bodies shivering uncontrollably. I'd try to move around, run in place, anything to bring back my body's core temperature. Sometimes if the guard felt extra sadistic, they wouldn't give you a towel to dry yourself, and you'd be bordering on hypothermia.

It was the opposite in the summertime. The indoor temperatures reached 120 degrees at times. Profusely sweating on a daily basis still didn't warrant more than the three allotted showers a week. At times, they didn't let you shower for whatever excuse. The jail could be on lockdown because of a problem, a fight, a stabbing, and then nobody got to move. Sometimes getting no shower could go on for weeks at a time, it just depended on the situation. The little sinks in our cell that we would use for fountain water would then become what we called a birdbath, and that would be our only means to clean ourselves.

This wasn't only solitary confinement in which we were treated in this manner. It was the entire prison system. In the other cells, if there were no shower, they'd take you to a shower to undress, and you'd stand in the bitter-cold shower stall naked, waiting for them to turn on the water. Sometimes the guards would leave you there, too, sometimes for up to an hour with or without a towel. It's not that these guards picked you personally, or just picked on you alone, they treated everybody that way.

The same sadistic treatment went for the toilet paper as well. If you asked for toilet paper because you ran out, you'd get ignored. Then if you asked a second time, they would tell you, "Shut the fuck up. I ain't giving you no toilet paper," and they don't bring you toilet paper. They purposely wouldn't bring it, but they acted like they forgot, and sometimes they'd wait for a change of shift so you'd be forced to sit there for another hour or so waiting to wipe yourself until someone showed mercy.

This was the hole for all of us, and it was designed to make us uncomfortable to keep us in line and not cause any more issues, but there was a fine line between abuse and punishment. They'd do things such as spit in your food right in front of you or steal or rip up our personal mail. By law, we must be seen once a week for medical. They would say they saw you but didn't. If an inmate actually was sick, they'd simply put your name on a sick call list and make you wait another week. These were just some of the games these perverted guards played with all the inmates. This type of treatment was what would cause inmates to have pent-up aggression and then retaliate.

Like everything, there was bad, and there was some good. There were a lot of decent guards at MCC, but then there were some insecure, deplorable pieces of shit. They were the ones who would ruin the peace, making it difficult for the guards who did their job professionally because they'd already hyped up and angered the prisoners.

The injustice at times was unbearable, and many men couldn't handle the isolation and horrid conditions. It was one thing to be confined and serving time, but it didn't mean any of us deserved to be tortured in the manner in which we were treated. All of us were like ticking time bombs, no one ever knowing how far any of us could be pushed before we'd snap. We each would snap in different ways, some lashing out in anger, others attempting to take their own life.

Greg DePalma was a made guy whose father was a captain in the Gambino family. He had started to rat, then decided he didn't want to cooperate anymore. He wound up hanging himself. Another guy, Louie Turra, was a Philly mobster who took his own life because he didn't want to rat. Turra's father had been killed while walking to get a chemo treatment. Later, Turra's own uncle wore a wire to bust his own nephew. The treachery was beyond belief, and no one gave a shit.

Then there was Nick Scarfo's son, who couldn't take the effects of the life either. He was in his mid-teens when he hung himself in his home. He was a vegetable forever, and then he finally died. I'd been a witness to so many men under mental duress and were unable to pull out of it, so they'd take their own life. It was one guy after another dropping out.

The difference between living through the nightmares on the streets as opposed to jail was that being in jail, one couldn't get away from the insanity. We were stuck in a hellhole, and if the guards had it out for you, they would find a way to get you. Even if one was on their best behavior, it wouldn't matter; sometimes the cards would be stacked against us no matter what.

One particular high-risk inmate was serving time at MCC in solitary confinement. He was Jeffrey Edward Epstein, and he was convicted for sex trafficking. He was found dead in his solitary cell. It was ruled a suicide when everyone knew that was a lie. He was killed, or he was helped with his suicide, courtesy of the guards who were able to cover up the truth. Absolutely no way was it suicide.

Most people would say it was due justice for Epstein, and maybe it was for what he did to innocent girls. The point was, though, to show how much power the guards have in the jail and what they were capable of accomplishing. We were helpless. There was no one to help control or regulate what happened on the inside. Everyone from the public sector was ignorant as to how much power the guards had in controlling life and death.

The story that was released to the papers said the jail's surveillance cameras were down. There were alarms and systems in place for when a camera would go offline, and then that prisoner must be immediately moved to a new cell within minutes. Plus, every shift was required to report the camera's outage until it was fixed.

In solitary confinement, we were watched twenty-four hours a day. One was never really left alone for more than fifteen minutes at a time, sometimes less. Authorities would come by, day and night, from lieutenants, the warden, regular guards, the captain of the solitary confinement cells, psychologists, and others. There were also frequent mandated tour passes at specific times in the solitary cell section.

It was almost impossible when they said a guy like Epstein could be successful in killing himself. He was a high-level inmate in solitary confinement and had just been on suicide watch. Those guards would never have put Epstein in a cell if the camera was not working. Absolutely impossible. It was a cover up.

The jail system wasn't the only place where made men would mentally lose it. There were made men from all over taking their lives because they could no longer take the effects the life was having on them. This life was a walking disaster, but people allowed themselves to get lured in for all the glamour, money, and prestige. When they found they no longer want to be part of the life, it would be too late. Things didn't work that way, and sometimes there was only one way out. They get to the point where they can't take the life that they're killing themselves.

I stayed in solitary for a while. I don't remember exactly how long it was, a couple of months, maybe. Being locked away in grimy, single-man cells for twenty-three hours a day was never easy.

I remember vividly the day I was transferred into my regular cell. It was September 11th, the day our country was attacked by extremists. The significance of being released on such a day showed me the guards cared in some way, showing a sense of vigilance for other Americans. Not only did they give me my privileges back, they dropped the assault charges against me. They were now feeling the same level of animosity I had been for these terrorists. I wasn't looked down upon on anymore by any of the authorities because they knew I respected our flag, our country, and our American soldiers.

Interestingly enough, it would be Ramzi Ahmed Yousef, the mastermind behind the bombing of the World Trade Center, who would soon wind up being incarcerated at MCC.

I'd get asked all the time by inmates why I relentlessly kept picking on terrorists. I told them it was their mindset. They'd been so severely brainwashed with hate and convictions that they could never change back to any level of humaneness.

I understood that when a person changed, they would abandon their beliefs and speak against the extremists and all the horrific things they did. There was only one terrorist who I thought could have changed for the better. His name was Zazi. His father was a hardcore terrorist, one who tried to bomb a building in Manhattan using a car bomb. His father would never cooperate and talk to the government, but Zazi did.

I would catch him several times crying in the corner of his cell. Even though there was nothing he could say that could stop me from detesting him, he at least would talk against the life of the extremists.

He told me he many times, "I'm not my father. I didn't want to do this. My father forced me to do this ever since I was a kid. I've been brainwashed to do this." A small part of believed he no longer wanted to be part of his father's organization.

BONUS CHAPTER

Ronald Turchi, Jr.

My name is Ronald Turchi, Junior. I first met Johnny Alite in Atlantic City, New Jersey, at one of the casinos. Johnny knew of my father, Ronald Turchi, who was the acting consigliere to the Philadelphia crime family. My father tried to keep me sheltered from the life as much as he could, but the more he did, the more I wanted to go the other way. The money was too great for me not to be there. Even though my father was a very important man, I refused to ride on the coattails of his name. Don't get me wrong, I enjoyed the benefits that came with our name. We could walk right into clubs and not wait in long lines. It was like everywhere we went, people would roll out the red carpet, treating us pretty much like movie stars.

For being a twenty-one-year-old kid in the late '80s and having experienced all the money and glam surrounding me, there was no way I was going to choose another path. I was young and impressionable, and I remember that when I was with Johnny, I felt ten feet tall. He was about five years older than me, and he was strong and confident, yet very humble and cordial. He was always ready to back up his reputation without hesitation, and soon, Philadelphia knew not to fuck with him.

Looking at him as a whole, no one would think him capable of the things he'd done, but looking deep into his eyes, I could tell he had already lived three lifetimes. It was interesting to watch John walk into a room. It was as if the seas parted when he came through. He just had that charismatic way about himself, where people would want to cling to him.

John had been driving down to Philadelphia more and more, wanting to spread his wings and expand his network further. I was enamored with how many money-making schemes he had going on all at the same time. I would soon find myself immersed in his world. We would prove to become great friends, and we would do a lot of business together over the years, from moving drugs, sports betting, shakedowns, loansharking, to setting up drug dealers and robberies.

John Alite and my father would grow close together as well, especially when they both served time together in Allenwood Prison, and then when they met again at a halfway house. My father would tell me stories about John and how wild and fearless he was, sometimes fighting against six guys at a time. I'd just shake my head in amazement. John would always look after my father in prison, and the level of trust and respect they had for each other was almost like father and son.

When my father got home after serving ten years from a RICO case, the Philadelphia mafia was falling apart. Too many things were going on all at once. Angelo Bruno had just been killed. He had been the boss of the Philadelphia crime family for two decades. Angelo Bruno's driver was John Stanfa, who was thought to have taken part of his own boss's murder. Angelo was shot with a shotgun in the backseat of a car while John Stanfa was driving. John had taken off for a while after the murder, but I don't remember how long he was gone for.

With Angelo Bruno having been killed, Nicky Scarfo stepped in to take the role of boss until he got locked up. After Nicky Scarfo went to jail, there weren't many men left to choose from except for a lot of young guys with no experience.

The entire mob was on shaky grounds, and when John Stanfa came back home, the Gambino family had appointed him boss. John was an old-time grease ball from Sicily and, just simply put, he was a motherfucker.

John Stanfa tried to pull everyone together to create a mafia that resembled the old times, but that era had been dead for a long time. Things changed all the time, the world is in constant change, and the future generations are never like the last. If one couldn't recognize the change of tides and alter their course, they would soon be left behind. Stanfa was too old-school. He had no clue he needed to re-structure protocols and policies for the day and age we were living in.

The drug business was where the money was at, and these men were going to step on people to get their piece of the pie. The guys on the streets didn't want to be told they couldn't flip drugs as they watched the boss sit back and make all the money while they took all the risk.

My father didn't want to be bothered by anything Stanfa did, and any opportunity Joey had, he'd be in my father's ear, saying, "Look at this fucking guy, Ron. How could we follow this guy? He's no good. He can't earn no money. He's greedy." Of course, Joey had won my father's confidence over; anyone could see Stanfa wasn't the right one to lead. I'd grown up with Joey, and everybody was always friendly with him. He had his own following who were ready to support and follow him anywhere.

Joey said to my father, "Let's get an approval from New York. Tell them what's going on and that we're not liking what Stanfa's doing. We explain everything to them, and then see what they say. They might shoot and kill us, or they might say they can't do a fucking thing and that we can't touch him."

There was nobody better than my father to make arrangements for a meeting in New York with the Gambinos. They knew he had the connections with the boss and the under boss for New York.

Many of the Gambino men had already served at least ten years in jail with my dad. He got very friendly with Nicky Corozzo while serving time. The problem was how my father was to get under-cover messages into the right hands. At the time, John Gotti Junior was in control of the Gambino family, and from my father's point of view, he was an imbecile who was clueless to mob business. My father wasn't going to send messages to Junior; he didn't trust him at all.

The only one my father could trust with this sensitive informa-tion was Johnny Alite. He was able to bypass Junior and hand-deliver those letters into the right hands. Johnny would eventually set up a face-to-face meeting between Philly and the Gambinos. Once the meeting was set up, my father, Joey, and a couple other gentlemen went into New York in hopes of getting things rectified. It was a dangerous meeting because they didn't know if they were going to walk out of there in one piece or get killed for requesting a hit on a Gambino-made boss.

New York's decision had been made at that very meeting. My father and Joey received the approval they needed to go after John Stanfa. Trying to push Stanfa out of the way would prove to be difficult. Philly would become a power grab that would spiral into an all-out war on the streets. There would be a shootout on every corner, guys getting killed left and right, and bodies flying all over the place. It was absolutely insane.

During this Philly war, Joey Merlino would be shot in a drive-by, but he would survive. There were ambushes on both sides, none of the men having regard if a family member was in harm's way or not. All bets were off in this war, and it would be Stanfa and his son who would get attacked on a local expressway. His son would be shot in the face three times, and it was a miracle that he would live through it.

One of the more tragic moments of the Philly split involved two brothers, Michael "Mikey Chang" Ciancaglini and Joey Ciancaglini. The brothers took opposing sides and wound up turning on each other. They would shoot through each other's home windows, even with the kids in the house. It was crazy. Mikey would wind up shooting his own brother multiple times for standing behind Stanfa. Joey would survive, but he would never be right again or able to walk. Mikey wasn't so lucky. He was later killed by one of Stanfa's crew, Billy Veasey, who then, in turn, got killed.

This life was not a life for the faint of heart. It was cold and ruthless. I knew these men who tragically died in the Philly split. Some of them were Louis DeLuca, Felix Bocchino, Jimmy "Brooms" Diaddorio, Fran Cesco, Rod Colombo, Mario Riccobene, Frankie Baldino,

Nicasio Zagone, Mikey Ice, and Duchy Alcohol, whose body was never found.

No one was able to take out Stanfa before he was convicted and sent to jail. With Stanfa in jail, New York then appointed a three-man commission for Philly. A boss, an underboss, and a consigliere. This was the moment when my father became consigliere for the Philadelphia mob.

John Alite was fairly laid-back during the Philly split. He was told by New York to not get directly involved in the murders and to stay out of the line of fire. It didn't stop him from expanding into the Philly area, though. Everybody else was treading carefully, afraid of what was going to happen next, but Johnny wasn't. He seized every opportunity before him and brought me along with him.

We started moving a lot of drugs together, and anybody who was selling drugs on the streets of Philly and was not involved with us was in for a rude awakening. Sports booking was the same way. If those businesses were not turning in their booking to us, then it was time for them to go, or they'd be putting their life in danger. Drugs, robberies, shake downs, taking over businesses—you name it, we did it.

Because of John's close relationship with my father, he had the green light to do whatever he wanted to do in Philly. For any business John did that involved a certain level of income, a percentage had to get kicked up to the three-man connection, which involved my father. It behooved everyone to let Johnny have free reign because the man knew how to make money and lots of it.

John wanted to know who was dealing drugs in the area and who was taking sports bets and not turning their percentage into the mob. I took action and put a couple of guys out there to find out who was moving big drugs.

My crew and I came across a kid who was dealing with a major pot dealer in the area. He was moving anywhere between four and five hundred pounds of weed a week. It was an absurd amount to me. I was shocked people could smoke that much pot.

John and me had this kid Max put in an order for two hundred pounds of weed. Max already knew the address where he was to pick it up. They told him to stop by next Tuesday night. With the date set, John and me then took over and planned the rest of the robbery.

Winter daylight savings time was in full swing, which worked to our advantage because it got dark early. When Tuesday late afternoon rolled around, we had everything in place. Johnny planned the entire thing as if he were an orchestral conductor. He had us get two cars on the street—I was driving one, and another one of our guys was driving the second car. Johnny had his own car, making for a third getaway. I parked up the street a bit and watched as John got out of his car with about three other guys trailing behind him.

I knew Johnny wasn't really familiar with South Philly the way I was. It just struck me funny that he wasn't worried in the least if all of us had to split in different directions if this robbery didn't go well. Johnny didn't care, and he went right into that house as if he owned it.

All I heard from the outside of the house he burst into was a lot of banging, screaming, yelling, and then it all stopped. A few minutes later, Johnny came out of the front door looking like Santa Claus with six trash bags slung over his shoulder. All I could do was chuckle as I watched him cross the lawn. He loaded two bags in my car, put two bags in his, and two bags went in the other getaway car. Later, John told me he left the guys tied up in the house and that they didn't even give him an ounce of trouble.

We had a really nice score from that robbery. We got a hold of five hundred pounds of weed. We wanted to flip it around real quick to get the money. We wound up selling the stash for about four hundred dollars a pound. Do the math.

The robberies...they were fun and exciting because they were quick money scores and nobody had to check in with anybody at that point because Johnny had a direct line with my father to do whatever he wanted. We'd throw Joey a nice cut, and he'd be happy.

My brother-in-law was talking to me one day about this kid in Cherry Hill who lived in a half-a-million-dollar home. He usually kept about fifty percent cash and fifty percent product on him all the time. He said he and his girl never worked a fucking day in their lives. He was moving about a thousand ecstasy a week and pulled in close to a hundred thousand in steroids every two or three weeks.

Cash was king. My brother-in-law gave me a tip-off, and he didn't even know it. It took Johnny about two weeks to map everything out. The fact that it was the month of June really worked to our advantage. June was when everybody wanted to get fit and juiced up for the summer. Johnny and I knew a couple of guys who owned gyms. We had them order an absurdly huge amount of steroids.

We knew the kid, Sean, had the money on hand, and we understood how the drug operation worked. Sean would be putting in that order for steroids, and we knew he would have to have "x" amount of money on hand. It would be a double score for us.

When it was time to do the robbery, Johnny had come down with two guys from Brooklyn. One of them was the son of a skipper from New York, and there was another guy. All three of them were dressed in full FBI gear. With the blue FBI jackets and the official badges they wore around their necks, they looked like real agents.

I stayed in the car as a lookout. I couldn't go in during the robbery because Sean knew my brother-in-law, and he'd know who I was.

Johnny and his two guys got out of the car and then rushed to the front door. When Sean opened the door, Johnny was flashing his badge, telling him he was FBI. They all went inside, and the door got shut. They were in there a good twenty minutes before Johnny came walking out with almost four hundred thousand dollars.

My brother-in-law was telling me about Sean being robbed. He wasn't happy about it because he had money involved with Sean. I had no idea he had put money up with the kid. I felt bad about the robbery at that point, but what was done was done.

When Sean called my brother-in-law, he was distraught and asking for his advice. He was going to call the agency to find out if they were in trouble or if they were going to just let them go. Then he asked, "Do you think the FBI is going to come back and lock me up?"

They were left with their wrists zip-tied together. Then they sat on the fucking floor in the middle of his living room for about a half-hour before it struck him that maybe he should try to untie them both.

"When do you ever know an FBI agent to kick down the front door, charge through your house, tie you up, and then rob you?" My brother-in-law assured him that it wasn't the fucking FBI. The kid was dumb as a doorknob, but he knew how to make money.

The crazy part about this story was that my brother-in-law suggested Sean reach out to me because I had connections. I could find out who robbed him. Seeing the opportunity, I said, "Yeah, sure. Tell him fifteen grand, and we'll find out who did it."

Sure enough, the kid came up with the money. I get some kid to go with me to face Sean and take the blame for the robbery. We gave him a fictitious name and a role play.

"When we're in front of Sean, I'm going to scream and yell at you," I explained. "Johnny might give you a little slap on the head or whatever. Then you're going to say, 'I blew the money.' We're going to tell you that you're never allowed to rob anyone ever again, and then we're going let you leave the room."

In the end, Sean was satisfied and impressed with our detective work. He wanted protection, so in order to get that, he would send us about five to ten thousand dollars a month. The idiot just set himself up.

Johnny was loving Philly and the ease at which he could rob and take over. He would say, "These guys are fucking soft as they come, you know? They're nothing like New York."

A group of Jamaicans living in north Philly were moving anywhere between four to five keys a week. I figured they had about four hundred thousand dollars on hand, plus any drugs they were selling in their stash house. This robbery was going to be a little stickier because there would be guns involved, and those Jamaicans were extremely vicious. This wasn't the young yuppie crowd dealing weed who didn't know how to fight back; these guys would shoot to kill.

This would require us picking out the right guys who knew what they were doing when confronting this level of violence, and then having the balls to carry through. The last thing we needed if something were to go wrong on the inside was for one of our men take off.

This was one of the few times we wore ski masks in a robbery. The Jamaicans and Mexicans came with cartels, and we didn't need their heat. We had a couple of drivers strategically parked near the Jamaicans' house, but it was Johnny, me, and this kid named Tommy who did the actual robbery.

As we busted through the front door fully armed and ready for fire, I was hyper-aware of everything at once. It was a real adrenaline rush. Two of the Jamaicans were completely taken off-guard when we broke in. A third man sat eerily calm at the kitchen table as if he'd been expecting us all along. He glanced at the loaded gun he had set on the table in front of him. He was debating whether or not to grab it, but Johnny didn't give him a chance to complete his thought before the butt end of John's shotgun was rammed into the side of his head. John moved swiftly as he swiped the gun from the table.

There were about three or four Jamaicans, and they were loaded for bear. They had stacks of machine guns lined along the walls and magazines on the counters.

We weren't dealing with small-time drug dealers; this was some serious business here. These were guys who were moving some serious shit. They'd shoot you, and they were ready to shoot it out on the street.

Tommy and me were holding the others at gunpoint while John set the lead. He was in complete control, walking in like it was nothing. It was sometimes amazing to watch him get ready for a robbery, strap on his gun, and just walk right in any establishment as if there were nothing to it, and then rob them.

John was making the calls and giving the demands. The guy righted himself in his chair, then said, "I'm going to get you, man." He drawled out the word "man" in a thick Jamaican accent, adding, "You bumbaclot," which means you're a used sanitary pad, a douchebag motherfucker.

Johnny pounded the end of the gun, full force into the side of his head. He did it in the blink of an eye, he was so fast. The man dropped to the floor with his head split open. It was then they knew Johnny was a cold-blooded killer and that we meant serious business. The other two guys then decided they'd better cooperate.

I didn't know at the time what it was with them using the term "bumbaclot," but I knew it was the worst thing one could be called by a Jamaican. After we tied the three of them up, we robbed them. There was about a hundred grand hidden in the refrigerator that we pulled out. Two of the guys were wearing Rolex watches, which we took for ourselves. It was still a good score, but we didn't come away with as much as we thought we would.

To me, it was pretty crazy because even though I was involved in a lot of robbery scenes with John, I still had to build myself up to get to his level of violence. I wasn't used to taking immediate action using extreme measures.

John was everything about being a hitman. Alite didn't need drugs, alcohol, or a pep talk to do what he did. He was always ready to go at the drop of a hat, able to go in any direction, and he fought anything coming his way.

Ronald Turchi, Jr., continued

Illegitimate businesses and criminal activities weren't the only ways John Alite and I made money. We took the life that we had, the people in it, all the connections, and we networked to create legitimate businesses. We were involved with a lot of businesses together, as well as having our own separate endeavors.

I had owned a nice bar in South Philly. I spent every day there, and I guess one could say it also served as a home base for having meetings and running my sports and horse betting business.

It must have been around twelve noon when this gentleman came in to sit at the bar. He'd been coming in everyday for a while now to have a few drinks and place some bets. He was a real nice guy, and we became quite friendly with each other. Art was his name. He was from Vermont, and it was apparent to all by the way he talked and held himself that he came from another side of the world.

I said hello and got him his usual drink, then went about my business. I had overheard him talking on his cell phone. "I can't believe they broke up another truck," he said, upset. "How are we going to get these jobs done?"

As I wiped out a glass with a clean towel, I stepped over to Tommy, who was working for me, and asked in a low voice, "What's going on with this guy?"

"I don't know." Tommy shrugged. "I think the union's fucking with him, breaking his balls and not letting him do some work."

After he ended his phone call, I went over to him. "Hey, Art. What's going on?"

"Ah, nothing," he said, waving me off.

I was really interested in knowing, and I really just had to ask, "What kind of business do you do?"

"Well, I'm in construction," he said, taking a sip of his drink. "I'm putting up cell phones sites."

"What do you mean?" I asked.

"Well, I'm building sites in Center City, and I can't even get my trucks on the job. The electrical unions are messing with me; they're breaking my trucks up. They busted all the windows in my trucks, and then they stole our tools."

"Really?" This took me by surprise. "Well, how much time do you need to finish the job?"

He pursed his lips in thought, then said, "It's only like four or five days. Especially when you go on the rooftops. It doesn't take that long."

I really liked Art, and it bothered me that he was having issues. I felt bad for him. I went back to Tom and said, "I think I'm going to help him out."

"What are you going to get out of it?" Tommy asked.

I shook my head and said, "No, it's not like that. He's just a nice guy. I want to see if I can help him out."

Flip phones were just really just starting to take off at this time. If someone didn't have a cell phone, they weren't anybody. Without a cell, one could no longer conduct business anymore. They would've been left behind the technological curve.

I went into my office and placed a call down to the city. I knew a business agent who was involved with the electrical union.

When he answered the phone, I said, "Carlo, It's Ronnie Turchi here. Listen, I need a favor."

"What's up?" he asked.

"I've got a guy down here who's putting up cell phone towers."

"Yeah, yeah, I know who he is," he interrupted. "That mother-fucker won't let us get involved with any of his business," he said. "We're going to shut him down until they get us involved. He's stealing a ton of our electrical work."

Philadelphia was a strong union town, and this man wasn't happy about the situation. "Look, do me a favor," I said. "I'm getting in good with this guy. I'll get him to come down, and we'll all talk. Maybe we can do something where we could put some electricians on his jobs, but right now, I need you to back off for four or five days so he can finish this job."

"All right, you got it, Ron," he said.

I walked back to Art and told him, "Hey, Art, could you get this job done in four days?"

His brows furrowed, curious as to why I cared. "Yeah, why?"

I leaned in, placing my elbows on the wooden bar. "Listen to me. Get everything done you need to do. You go down to the site tomorrow…"

He cut me off and said, "Forget it." He shook his head. "It's impossible."

"Just listen to me, Art," I said, trying to convince him. "Go down there in the morning. Nobody's going to break your balls. Nobody's going to have a picket line. You'll be fine, but you have four days to get it done."

He was looking at me like I was completely out of my mind. I just grinned at him. Helping people, including strangers, was something me, my father, and John did a lot of. Maybe that was one of the reasons why we got along so well. We were always rooting for the underdog, the people a little less fortunate.

After the day was done, I had already forgotten all about Art. The next evening, Art came rushing into the bar. "Who the fuck do you know?" he asked, bewildered. "Do you want a job?"

I burst out in laughter. "Art, you know," I said with a smile. "Keep that in your back pocket. But if I can help you out in any way, I will. A fifty-thousand-dollar-a-year salary wasn't worth my time. I was making a minimum of five thousand a week. It wasn't too long afterward, however, that I'd be asking if Art's job offer still stood.

So much was going on all at the same time. Mob boss Joey Merlino got locked up, John Stanfa was causing problems, and no one was doing anything on the streets. The FBI was all over the place, and all of a sudden everything just shut down, and I was no longer making the money I was used to.

When Art gave me the job, he wanted to know if I knew anybody in New York so he could expand. I laughed. "Did I know anyone in New York?" I repeated, enthusiastic. "Yeah, I've got contacts," I told him.

I found I was very mechanically inclined. I was on a rooftop in New York sketching sites when Art saw my sketching abilities. At that point, I became deeply involved with the inner workings of the company and quickly became the go-to guy.

When Johnny Alite got involved with us, he came up with new ideas for us to expand. We teamed up with a crane business in Philadelphia, locking down the market. We controlled many cranes in the area and made massive amounts of money because they were expensive to use.

We told construction companies they weren't using any other crane company but the ones we told them to. With me being involved with my father's connections, we had the influence and power to shut down unions and union sites.

Anytime we needed a crane, we were getting a piece of the action. With over four thousand sites using these cranes on a daily basis, one could imagine the profits. Other than shutting the crane companies down, it was nice to be able to run a business legitimately.

Cell tower business was booming with Nextel, Verizon, and Sprint, which were all major companies. Unfortunately, with this line of work, we needed to have big money to stay afloat. It would cost anywhere between forty and fifty thousand for us to do one cell tower site, and the payment for the finished job wouldn't come in until ninety days later. When Sprint or Nextel wanted to give us another job, we had to be ready to roll. We had to have the working capital. By taking on three to five sites a month, we'd spend almost two hundred grand or more out of our pockets before we'd receive payment for the job. It was a constant money chase.

It was so stressful trying to stay afloat in the beginning. I had taken out a street loan to help cover operating costs, and months later, I was still covering a three-thousand-dollar-a-week loan that had no end. The loan sharks were charging exorbitant prices. I didn't want anyone to know what I had done, not even my father. I wanted to handle my own business, but somehow John had found out about it.

John was ticked off because he knew those shylocks were trying to control me and keep me in debt. He gave me about a hundred grand to pay off the loan, then took it a step further by making a personal visit. John basically slammed the money down on the loan shark's desk and told them my debt was paid. That was it. Everything was settled that quick. No one argued with John.

John and I were basically controlling the entire city. Anything that came into the city was ours. No one could go behind our backs. If someone put a crane up in the air on a construction site, within a day, somebody would be calling to tell us about it. Word on the street was that we'd pay easy money just for tipping us off so we could go after a crane job.

No one could stop us. And because the fact that I had a unique connection with my father's position in the mafia, we had control of the unions, and we were shutting them down. I was making so much money, gangsters and my father alike thought I was nuts for still running the streets.

They all told me to get out of the life. It was a perfect out for the amount of income being generated, but I wanted to play businessman by day and be gangster by night. It worked for a while, but burning the candle at both ends would soon catch up to me. We were growing so big and expanding so fast, we had to bring on legitimate companies that could handle the workload for us to remove some of the pressure.

"Ron," my mother said over the phone, "your father wants to talk to you." I knew what she meant. My father wanted to meet in person. My father hated the phone and would cut you off just to hang up. The phone was what helped authorities put my father in jail years prior because of wiretaps on the phones.

"Okay, I'll probably be home early. I don't have any plans for tonight." I figured it was nothing too important. Maybe he needed to talk about the cranes or the cell phone business. "I should be home around eight or nine o'clock. Tell daddy I'll see him then."

I had my own apartment but still spent a lot of nights at home with my parents. I had been out late the last couple of nights, and I was tired, so I had every intention of going home. A couple guys wound up stopping by my apartment later in the day just to hang out. We wound up having a couple drinks, and then someone asked, "Hey, who wants to go out?" I had apparently found my second wind, so I decided to head out with my friends to the local bar.

It was probably about nine when my mother called me on my cell. "I thought you were coming home. You know, daddy's been waiting for you." I could tell she was a little irritated.

"Yeah, all right. I'm just having a few drinks with a couple guys. I'll be home later on, I promise," I said, trying to appease her. I had every intention of getting home early, but I let time slip away from me.

I walked into my parents' house about two in the morning to find my mother asleep on the sofa. I gently nudged her shoulder and whispered, "Mom, why don't you go on to bed?"

When she realized it was me nudging her, she became fully awake. "What the hell, Ron?" she said, ill-tempered. "Your father was waiting for you the entire night."

"Look, I know...One thing led to another, and I lost track of time. Wake me up tomorrow morning before daddy goes into work," I said.

"Fine, I'll tell your father in the morning."

The next morning, I slept in late; no one ever one woke me up. I made my way downstairs and found my mother in the kitchen. "Hey mom, where's daddy?" I asked.

"Oh, he already left, but he said he'd meet you downtown." She turned around with a cup of coffee in hand, then added with disappointment, "You know, your father waited for you all night. You always say you're gonna come home, but you don't. You never do the right thing." No matter how old I am, I will always love and respect my parents. I knew she was just being a mother who cared.

"All right, all right," I said, "I'll catch up with him downtown. He's my number one priority today." I picked up the phone and called him. "Dad, I'm coming down there, where are you going to be?"

"Don't worry about it," he clipped. He wouldn't even talk on the phone about the simplest of things. "I'll get up with you a little bit later. I'll let you know."

"That's fine, but mommy said you've been wanting to talk to me." I pushed him, curious to know what was so important.

"Look, I will talk to you when I see you. It'll probably be around twelve noon."

"Dad, what's going on? What'd you want?"

"Not on the phone," he said curtly. "I told you I'll talk to you later."

My dad had a little fish company on 13th and Bigler. This was our main place we hung out. I kept checking my watch because twelve o'clock came and went as I waited. Then one and two o'clock passed by with no sign of my father. My father wasn't one to stand me up. He wasn't answering his cell, but that didn't mean much of anything since he hated the phone so much. I figured maybe he got held up in a meeting or got behind schedule. He was always bouncing around from place to place.

He was also known to jump in the car and take a ride to Atlantic City on occasion. He'd disappear for hours at a time to gamble. There were a handful of times he'd get lucky at the casinos, and if he was on a winning streak, he'd be known to stay there for eighteen hours straight. He was just that kinda guy. By the evening, my mind was spinning, and my mother was worried. He would have at least made some kind of contact with us by now.

I had later found out that a couple days before my dad went missing, Roger Vella had told my father he needed to meet up with somebody. There were a couple of meetings and sit downs he had to attend that day, but I didn't know what meeting would've been his last. I found out later that John Alite warned my father about a few things, and one warning was not to go to one of those meetings. I didn't want to think the unthinkable, that someone had set him up to be killed.

It was a gut-wrenching time in our lives, and with each day that passed with no sign of my father, the days became bleaker and more discouraging. All I wanted to do was find him because I'd seen it where no bodies get found. I believe that would've been harder for me to live with.

It would be three days later that we'd get the call from one of the detectives we'd been working with. It would be impossible for me to describe all the emotions that surged through me all at once. I was frozen in an abyss of torment and agony as I listened to the detective give us his statement. Receiving and digesting the news was like being struck by lightning, knocking the life out of me.

The authorities found my father's car down the street from a restaurant we had owned years before. Someone had reported a foul smell coming from the trunk of a car. The authorities called a tow company and hauled the vehicle to the police station. I guess that is where the forensics team had opened the trunk of the car to find my father brutally murdered. He was hogtied and shot to death, then stuffed in the trunk of his own car.

It would be within minutes after we spoke with the detective that the news media would have my father's death on display for the world to see. The death of the consigliere for the Philly mob would be blasted over the TV, radio, newspapers, and other outlets. To the world, he was just another mafia man, a consigliere who was murdered, but to me, he was my father, my rock.

It was determined by the coroner his time of death was between twelve and twelve thirty in the afternoon. That was the time he was supposed to meet me, and that was ultimately what took him to his death.

What would haunt me for years afterwards was not knowing what my father wanted to tell me. I'd never know, and that is where much of my pain comes from. Did he want to tell me something important, something for only me to know? I didn't want to believe it was anything other than needing to discuss the crane operation.

I knew my father's death hurt Johnny a lot. He loved my father. They spent time together in jails and halfway houses. They were close in their own right for the things they went through together in jail.

Our cell phone business was becoming an enormous operation, but then the fucking bottom fell out. I got indicted, and Johnny went on the run. Both of our lives were in danger, and where I was being held, I couldn't even get word to John to get his advice.

"This is not your life," the memory of my father's voice echoed over and over in my head, "This is not your life—this is mine."

He chose his path, and he owned it. He knew the risks, and so did I, but I just thought we were invincible. I threw my head back in anger and frustration.

"Fuck," I yelled out in exasperation. "How the fuck did I get where I'm at?" Now I was smack in the middle of hell, and there was no way out.

CHAPTER 21

The Alite Empire

Alite was buying machine guns, semi-automatics, shot guns, hand-guns, and whatever else he could get his hands on. The main reason was, in his mind, that he wasn't going to wind up dead like so many of his close friends and associates and other men in the life who he knew on a personal basis.

The empire that John had built was at its pinnacle. He owned three houses in Queens, a piece of property in Manhattan one block from the Twin Towers, two houses in Princeton, New Jersey, and then the fifteen acres in Cherry Hill with three houses on it. His driveway in Cherry Hill was five blocks long. John had twelve fighter dogs consisting of Pitbulls, Mastiffs, Dobermans, and Rottweilers.

Besides the drugs, sports betting, parking companies, robberies, and extortion, John lent money all over the street as a shylock. The legitimate businesses he owned were also a testament to his business acumen.

He owned a very profitable parking company based in Tampa and two very hot night clubs in Florida called American Cowboy and Stampede. He owned the Coliseum in South Jersey in 1994. It was a big workout facility that housed an Olympic-sized pool, gym, and daycare. The Philadelphia Flyers used to practice hockey at the Coliseum. In addition, Alite owned two glass companies and their buildings, having bought them outright.

As mentioned earlier, his fifteen acres in Cherry Hill was for his and his family's personal use. He turned the property into a sports complex. He added baseball cages, an outdoor boxing ring, a pavilion gym with an outdoor pool, and trikes and go-carts so people could ride around his lake and property.

Many people would think that with all of my legitimate business, why couldn't I quit and step away from the life while I was ahead?

Yes, I had the foresight and intelligence to be a brilliant moneymaker, legal or not, but leaving the life didn't work like that.

No matter how much time passes, there would always be too many enemies who still wanted to either kill me, hurt me, or destroy me. The minute one quits and leaves the streets, they lose the ability to keep their ear to the ground, and then you lose connections. You always have to be in the game, always keeping your hooks in, and always making money for others, which helps keep them loyal to you.

My endless connections and ability to reach to anyone for help outside of New York and into almost any country was astounding to even me. I have more hooks than anyone around the world. Of course, that came from all the money I made guys, me being good to them, and me not breaking my ties to them through the good and bad times. I still have loyalists in all the mafia families, although none of us announce it.

The older I got, I found I handled things with more patience, trying to be smarter. I learned to control my expressions and body language so as not to show what was really on my mind.

I realized I needed to adapt to each era and generation I was living in, then I needed to accomplish what I wanted. I needed to figure out how to get there without always killing like I did before. My enemies could sit and wait days, weeks, months, or years for me to seek retribution. Instead of using violence, my attacks would now come in many different ways, and they would come.

Remember the mind rules the roost.

CHAPTER 22

End of and Era

The biggest blunder in mafia history was the murder of Gambino mob boss Paul Castellano. He ran the Gambino family as a business and a corporation, intelligently and quietly within the Gambino faction. It would be Gotti Senior who put the hit on Paul Castellano, and everyone knew it. Gotti stepped right in and took over as the new boss. Gotti was first introduced into the mob through Angelo Ruggiero, who was Aniello Dellacroce's nephew.

Once the power got taken out of the Gambino faction's hands, guys like Peter Castellano, Paul's brother, would show up at the club. Peter was not a tough guy. After the murder, he'd go to the club and play a game of cards called Continental with Senior. He simply fell in line behind Gotti Senior like everyone else, even after Senior killed his own brother. One night he lost two hundred thousand dollars at cards. It seemed like he lost on purpose to get in good with Senior.

John Gotti Senior wasn't really ever going to get away with killing off Castellano. He was eventually going to get killed. There was no time clock for us when it came to revenge. There would be a lot of plots on killing Senior that people don't really know about. The FBI had wire taps everywhere, and a lot of guys went to jail for trying to plot and kill Gotti. The bottom line was, if he didn't go to jail, he was going to get killed eventually.

Gotti was a media disaster to the mafia being exposed, which gave rise to the instability and decline of the Gambino family. The biggest problem was that the mafia was starting to become a father and son union. Guys that had no business and didn't deserve to be straightened out were being straightened out just because their father was a big earner. Because they earned a ton of money, they started bringing their sons in. Those kids never knew what it was like, nor had to spend one day on the street. They were spoiled white rich kids who grew up with full privileges and a loaf of bread under each arm. That's not gangster. They're completely clueless of the street.

Guys like Jo-Jo Corozzo, who became the consigliere; Ronnie One-Arm, and his son Al, both captains, all got made in the Gambino family. This was what the reality of the mob hierarchy had become.

John Alite had hurt, shot, and robbed all kinds of made men throughout the years, and no one had taken retaliation or retribution against him. That led John to understand that the really tough guys, the guys who were true Cosa Nostra, were history. There was nobody left except a handful of guys.

Alite explains as only he can:

They were afraid because they were cowards, full of double standards and backstabbing liars who disgraced the forefathers of the mafia.

This was what destroyed the power within the Gambino family. Most of the made men under Senior's reign were useless idiots. Those men weren't capable of doing anything, and the Gotti faction would eventually pay with their lives for not retaliating when they should have. They would pay the price in history for being weak.

What people could never understand or see was the behind-the-scenes of our lives and who we really were behind closed doors. They had no realization of what had become of the mafia. People think when they hear "made guy" or "captain" that it is someone of high stature, but the '70s and '80s are gone. We are now a far cry from Fat Andy Ruggiano, captain of the Gambino family, who was made by men like Albert Anastasia. Ruggiano was made alongside Carlo Gambino and Albert Anastasia, true gangsters, real Cosa Nostra.

This was what became of the Gambino family. It fell like the fall of Rome. It's really important for people to see what the fuck had been going on with who and why, and where the streets stand now in this day and age. People need to know the difference between today's mafia men and old-school gangsters and killers like Johnny Carneglia who were true gentlemen, quiet, and low-key gangsters and businessmen—guys like Jimmy Brown, Tommy Gambino, Joe Gambino, Joe Piney, and Joe Gallo, who was the one-time consigliere of the family. Those men were true gentlemen.

I was done with them all. I was moving my own way, and I didn't care about any of them anymore because I saw what they were really about. I was going against the hierarchy of the Gambino family, and I was going to have my hands full.

CHAPTER 23

On the Run

Alite was released from jail in 2002 and had criminal cases coming at him from all directions. A lot of people in the life were cooperating, and John knew he was exposed because he had performed so many killings and shootings. Things didn't look good for John at all, and the walls seemed to be closing in on him. It would only be a matter of time before the authorities would catch up to John and the empire would crumble.

I wasn't willing to lose everything I built for me and my family. I could recognize when the end was near, and I was prepared.

Before I went on the run, I had a talk with my father. I said, "Dad, we have to talk about something." I drove him to a lake in Vorhees, New Jersey, off Route 561. It's a big lake that I used to jog around.

"I know I'm in trouble here," I said as we walked around the lake. My father didn't really understand. He didn't think I had all the trouble I had because I chose not to tell him.

"I think you're jumping the gun," he said, rambling on about what he thinks. He wasn't schooled enough in the street to understand. My family didn't know anything about all the things I was involved in. They didn't understand the intricacies of the crimes and RICO laws and all the other complicated things. My dad tried his best to tell me not to go, but he knew my mind was made up.

"Junior is weak. I had always thought he'd go in and talk," I said, gazing out over the lake. I turned to my dad and said, "He's separate. He's doing what his father did, blaming everyone for everything."

At this time, Junior and me were at each other's throats. I had discovered long before this point in time that he had been telling everybody to go to the police and testify against me. I didn't trust anyone, and I figured that whatever information Junior had, he was eventually going to give it up on me—or he already had, and now he's leaking it out.

I discussed other plans I had with my father and told him, "You can't trust anybody. Not one guy," I emphasized. There were too many guys who were talking, and there were too many shootings and killings I was involved with.

"We're going to do it this way," I said, looking at my father through my dark shades. "I'm not going to tell anybody I'm leaving or when I plan on leaving. I'm not saying anything to the kids, I'm not saying anything to my mother, I'm not saying anything to anyone. I'm just going to say goodbye, kiss them, and tell my son I had to go." I knew doing that would be easier said than done, but I had to do it. It was awful.

"I'm not going to tell you initially as to what country I'm going to, then after that, if I think it's too dangerous, I'm not going to tell you at all. So don't ask me what country I'll be in if I don't tell you." I could tell he didn't like not knowing where I was going to be, but he understood.

"Just in case they're all listening to the phones, I'm going to give you lies and tell you I'm in this country or that country when I'm actually not. I've given my email address and Facebook accounts to certain people who are spread across the globe to send out emails and Facebook messages to throw the authorities off my trail. Nobody would be able to figure out if it was really me or not. If it was me who wrote you an email, I'll tell you I did over the phone." My father didn't know much about computers, so he was going to have to ask my sister for help.

"Here's what we're going to do now," I said to my dad. "We're going to hit twenty phone booths, just me and you, and we're going to mark them down with the addresses so you know where they're at. I'm going to number them, and then we're going to have a system. When I call you for the first time on one of the phone booths, we'll decide what one that will be. After we finish that call, I'm going to give you a couple of numbers." I paused, letting him digest everything. "Let's say I'm going to tell you 'seven, two' over the phone. That means you go to phone booth number seven at two p.m."

I was also worried about undercover agents following my dad on the days we'd talk from a distance. If he made a straight dash to the phone booth, they'd figure out what he was doing pretty quick. They would then tap the pay phones and start monitoring them. I had known for a long time that the public phones were always tapped; it was how the authorities got a lot of mob cases.

I told my father he had to make sure he wasn't followed. I instructed him to go to a store or supermarket way before our scheduled time. Then when he'd come out with a bag of groceries or merchandise, he'd go to the phone booth and pretend to make a phone call. There would be nothing out of the ordinary about anyone performing that action.

Most of the booths I chose were local, within a fifteen minutes' drive from my dad's house. I also decided I needed at least five phone booths that were further out of range. I knew the ones further away would be safer. I would use those phones to convey something extremely important or serious, and then we wouldn't use that phone again until two months later. The authorities would never hold a phone that long if they tapped into it. I also picked a handful of phone numbers that would serve for the long-term and starred them.

CHAPTER 24

Alite Prepares to Leave His Family

I had actually been preparing for this moment a year because I saw the end was near. Over the past twelve months, I had been sending money to my cousin in Albania to hold for me, and I started shooting money into Canada into a bank account a couple years beforehand. I sent money to some of the guys who worked for me and made arrangements for them to be able to send me money wherever I was going to be. As far as all my businesses, I had taught my father how to run and handle them, and then I put him in charge of all my money, bills, and accounts.

When I first left, I took about sixty thousand dollars cash with me, then drove from New York to Florida where I would get a new passport. I was still on parole when I got the passport, so they shouldn't have given it me, but they did. I wasn't supposed to leave the country either, but I did that, too.

I went to St. Lucia under the guise that I was going on vacation. From there, I went to Cuba and wound up making a connection with a guy named Ron Ryan and his family, who ran a hotel on the beach. I got very friendly with them, and they helped me get established. I had set up some apartments up in Cuba using the Canadian bank system to pay for them.

I wasn't thinking this setup would be my life forever. I was hoping, in my mind, that I was going to live in Cuba and get citizenship, but I needed two hundred fifty thousand dollars to buy a property. I figured I would live there and then have my kids come visit me as soon as I thought it was safe enough. My original plan was not to run all over the world, but it ended up turning out that way.

Because of the cartel's son Andre LaFlore, who I had helped in jail by protecting him, I wound up getting in touch with the father because I knew he would help me. My next jump was to Colombia. The cartel had a matrix of bosses spread out, just like we did in the mafia. It would be another cartel boss who would help me out as a favor to LaFlore's father.

I never felt like I feared for my life in Colombia. The cartel faction I was living among were amazing people; all of them pitched in and helped me. They even let me know when immigration was looking for me with Interpol. They were looking out for me and moving me to different places I needed to stay to avoid Interpol.

When I was there during my stay with the cartel, I met two guys named Marty and Arthur, who both helped me move to Magdalena and then to Cali, Colombia. Those two men had given me more connections than I could ever have imagined. Once when Interpol was looking for me, they drove me from Colombia across to Venezuela and into to an army base to keep me hidden.

Marty and Arthur had me stay with a woman who was in the army and living on the army base. Looking back, I would've been safe there for a very long time if I hadn't moved around. No one bothered me there, but I ended up moving. I thought I was being too idle.

I met a man named Andre from San Andrés, an island off the coast of Colombia. He was a big mover of coke. Everywhere I went, I was building more and more connections. I had started boxing at Billy's Gym in Barranquilla, then I got involved in competitions all over, using it as an excuse to travel to other places like Venezuela, Valencia, and Caracas. The cartel would drive me across the borders and get me through all the checkpoints. We would ride in a caravan packed full of a dozen men or more. There must have been twelve different checkpoints from Barranquilla to Venezuela, and every time the guards stopped us, they never once looked at my passport. I simply gave the cartel the money to pay them off.

Eventually, I left for Europe, and from there, I went to Paris, Amsterdam, Belgium, Albania, Greece, Rome, Milan, and different places in Italy. I later went to Argentina, Uruguay, Paraguay, Canary Islands, West Africa, then Brazil. I bought six passports through Klaus, who was my connection in West Africa. Each passport had false names and different IDs, as I'd take different pictures of myself dressed in different clothing and jewelry. I was just cutting my hair, dying my hair different colors—black, brown, blond—and changing the style of it. In Jamaica and the Cayman Islands, I would dreadlock or cornrow my hair, using extensions so they could braid it. Once I would have to take off to Germany because Interpol was hot on my tail.

There must've been over twenty countries I went to, and throughout those countries, I had set up money trails, which gave me access to money in different locations and countries. Each place I went, I would give my connections my personal email and Facebook credentials so they could access my accounts. I told them once a week to use a different place to email my family, then write them as if it were me writing the letter. When I was in Albania, I told my cousin do the same thing. I had all these people doing emails for me in my name throughout all parts of the world to throw off the authorities.

One of the biggest obstacles I faced was getting myself set up and familiar with each country and their systems. I was going to other cities and setting up apartments where it was cheap. Some places like Cuba, I could get an apartment for two hundred a month. This would allow me to be able to jump from place to place at a moment's notice. I'd stash money, supplies, clothing, and passports in each place. Once things were established, I would travel from one place to the next, making it appear as if I were vacationing by only spending a few days at a time there.

While I was on the run, so many things were going on back home. I had associates and made guys who were piling on against me. I knew more and more guys were cooperating, and because of that, I was preemptive. I hired lawyers to help me out long before

I would ever be indicted. Some of the cooperators were guys like Ronnie One-Arm; Fat Dom; Joe Massino, boss of the Bonanno crew who wore a wire; Mikey Scars, Junior's right-hand man and a proven top government witness; and over twenty-five associates. They had all given me up.

Besides ratting on me, guys like Jimmy Cadicamo, who ran my night club, had been robbing me blind. Everybody thought for certain I was never coming back. Since I was gone, who better than me to start pointing fingers at and robbing? My hands were tied, and the only choice I had was to keep moving and covering my tracks.

No one ever wants to leave their family

BONUS CHAPTER

Claus

The old adage that "birds of a feather flock together" is a truism in many walks of life. In the illegitimate world, criminals can have a global connection that turns their felonious activities into millions upon millions of dollars.

Malmqvist, from a good middle class family in the suburbs of Copenhagen, grew up in a household that destined him for a legitimate life of honest hard work. He was brought up in a house that was built by his grandfather, with his two older sisters and both parents. His mother owned a small candy shop, and his father ran a tax office in the town hall where they lived. Claus did very well in school, having a keen, sharp mind, especially in mathematics.

Malmqvist departed from his loving and conservative family, becoming attracted to the housing projects near his town. In his words, the "concrete jungle" lured him into the drug and contraband trade, and inexplicably, the nice boy from a good Dutch family would become arguably one of the biggest drug dealers in Europe.

Sometime in 1992, Claus moved permanently to Spain to stay closer to the source of drug trafficking in Europe.

That year, through mutual friends in California, John Alite came in contact with Claus.

Malmqvist dealt in cocaine, cannabis, and hashish shipping from Spain to California, and he sent the illegal drugs via truck and, according to John Alite, "a hundred other different ways."

A Danish drug lord was convicted of smuggling 13 tons of hashish into Denmark on Monday in the country's biggest cannabis case.

Claus Malmqvist, 40, was sentenced to 16 years in prison, the maximum for drug crimes under Danish law.

Malmqvist, who had pleaded not guilty, appealed the ruling by the Copenhagen City Court, his lawyer Henrik Dupondt Joergensen said.

The court said prosecutors had proved that Malmqvist organized the transport of thirteen tons of hashish from Morocco to Denmark in 2003. Police had evidence of the transport, though they were not able to seize the drugs before they were sold.

The court seized ten million kroner (£1.3 million; $1.9 million) from Malmqvist, which authorities had traced to the hashish sale.

Claus was also convicted of attempting to smuggle five hundred kilograms (eleven hundred pounds) of cocaine from South America. That operation was aborted, police said.

Malmqvist was arrested in the Brazilian city of Belem in January 2005 and was extradited to Denmark nineteen months later.

Some thirty people have been convicted in the case on charges ranging from murder to extortion and money laundering.

Claus and I have known each other for thirty-plus years, since around 1990, and spent time together in a Brazilian prison. I consider him a good friend. This guy was the biggest Danish gangster in Europe. Pot, pills, hash—he did it all. He's a big guy, six foot five, with long hair. I call him the Nordic Narcos, as he once had two ships full of drugs. There is a television series being worked on now about his life and how we know each other and the things we did together; it's even called Nordic Narcos.

When I was on the run, Claus was able to, through connections he had with family and friends in Spain, keep me hidden. A guy named Ramon put me up for a time. He also used travel agencies to move me around so I didn't have to talk to regular people. A connection in West Africa gave me five passports. Good ones. Knowing the consiglieres in different countries further helped to make the necessary contacts.

Claus and I have traveled to Brazil, Germany, Spain, Morocco, but when I was in the Brazil prison, Claus's sister came to the prison, and I said, "What are you doing here?" It turned out her brother, Claus, was there, too. I said, "Well, he'll be with me soon." Claus spent sixteen or seventeen years in prison there.

In Brazil, we would go to the HELP discotheque, aka girls/prostitutes nightclub. It's in Rio de Janiero. We only went a few times because we didn't want to be recognized.

Claus and I are still friends, and we travel all over together. They are in production now and filming "Crime Watch" in Denmark, Sweden, and various places around the world. Now, it's like a reunion.

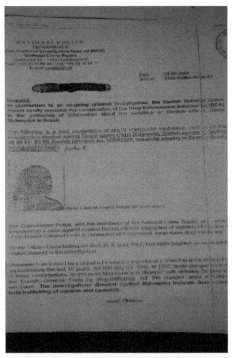

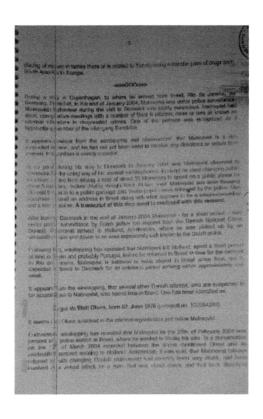

CHAPTER 25

Ronnie One-Arm Rats

The chickens come home to roost. Or was it the rats coming home to nest?

It was when Ronnie One-Arm made his opening statement in court that he broke the code of silence. Regardless of if anyone had given him permission to, our laws were our laws, and he was not allowed to admit to the existence of the mafia, but he did. He also wasn't allowed to admit positions held within the mafia, which he also did, revealing the fact that he was a captain in the Gambino family. Those very two things made him a rat.

He ratted on Vincent Asaro, a captain from the Bonanno crime family. He testified against him for being in control of a crew of guys called the Young Guns, who had committed countless robberies and murders. Vinny Asaro was charged, too, in connection with the famous Lufthansa heist, along with his close friend, Jimmy Burke. Ronnie One-Arm also wasn't supposed to blame other made members, and he did that in his opening statement.

By the time Ronnie One-Arm took the stand, I was in a Brazilian prison fighting to stay alive. I actually gave Ronnie permission to say I was in a drug business because if Ronnie beat the case, that meant they couldn't extradite me back to the United States.

UNITED STATES DISTRICT COURT, MIDDLE DISTRICT OF FLORIDA, TAMPA DIVISION, UNITED STATES OF AMERICA, Plaintiff, Case No. 8:04-CR-348-T-24TGW -vs- 18 October 2006, Tampa, Florida. EXCERPT OF TRANSCRIPT OF TRIAL PROCEEDINGS

SNIPPETS OF MR. TRUCCHIO'S TESTIMONY:

"Also, they said in 1984, which I can't understand why I'm here, it was Johnny Alite and John Gotti, Jr. If that's where this Indictment started, why am I here? Is there something wrong with that? I scratched my head, okay Johnny Alite and John Gotti, Jr., started a drug business. Okay, this is where we're building the foundation of the house from. They started the drug business. They worked in the drug business. Now, all of a sudden I come in. I'm hands on. Ladies and gentlemen of the jury, I've been followed almost every day of my life by the FBI. I know them by first-name basis, almost. Petroski, uh, McCabe -- who passed away -- Carillo, Organized Crime Task Force in New York. They came in my social club thousands of times playing cards. I -- they're going to show you a lot of pictures and stuff. Yes, I did know Johnny Alite. But in life you know people, they go their way and I go mine. After -- after the mid-nineties if I seen him to say hello, it was a lot. I -- I paid for my crimes, what happened. I don't know why they're throwing me in this. Maybe 'cause they couldn't get John Gotti, Jr. out of New York; New York wanted him too much. Just give me a second, please." (Pause.) "And do you want to know something? The truth of the matter is, John Alite is a thug. Johnny Alite, there was a falling out with him and John Junior."

"Johnny Alite went to jail. In jail he met people from Philadelphia and Atlantic City. He wound up hanging out with the New Jersey mob, then came to Florida. He stole all these businesses from every person. You think he would gave me a penny? He didn't give me a quarter; not a penny, not one red cent. Not one red cent did I get. And I swear that on my other arm that I should lose the use of it. Not one red cent."

Not only was Ronnie's opening statement giving me up, but later, he said he was afraid I was going to kill him.

"And all of these crimes started in New York. Do you think the FBI in New York is going to give me a free pass? Why, because I'm good looking, I'm pretty? Why? They ain't going to give me a free pass, they're going to lock me up. This is from 1984. If this is the kind of criminal enterprise that I was running there, New York's FBI got to be the stupidest people in the world. The Organized Crime Task Force of New York got to be the stupidest people in the world. The Queens District Attorney's detectives have to be the stupidest people in the world. The Brooklyn District Attorney's Office has to be the stupidest people in the world. They've got thousands of hours of tapes; they're going to show you selective ones, ones that benefit them. And the ones -- you see, the Government can get more than I can get. The tapes that I need to show and prove, can't get "em. It's not pertinent to the case. But it is. Because they're going to show people -- and there's other tapes that show me with other people after this."

"Excuse me for a minute." (Pause.) "Oh, like I said, all these here crimes, most of them started in New York. Just think, you know, my six-year-old daughter will probably say, well, if all those crimes are committed in New York, and those are 16, 20 years ago, why is it here now in Florida they're prosecuting him? I keep on scratching my head every day. I'm losing my hair more."

THE COURT: Mr. Trucchio, don't argue.

MR. TRUCCHIO: Oh. Oh, okay, sorry.

THE COURT: Just --

MR. TRUCCHIO: "Well, the foundation was John Gotti, Jr. and Johnny Alite. All the crimes were committed in New York. Now we're here. And you mean New York never solved any of the crimes? It took Florida to find out about crimes that happened in New York? No, ladies and gentlemen. People were tried and Convicted or pleaded out to those crimes. But I wasn't involved in New York. So, New York once again liked my pretty little face: You go home, you good boy. You don" have to be charged."

"Why didn't they charge me? Miraculously they found witnesses from that cesspool to come in and trade their freedom for my life. And, you know, when we talking about being judged, whatever religion we have and we believe in, we're going to be judged by the true guy. And, you know, the people that think they're doing good, they going to be surprised when they say, no, not you, you go down. You did a bad thing. They think they're doing good things. Lying and deceit is not good. How come I wasn't locked up on any of them cases in New York and people went to jail on them? Other alleged capos from different crime families. Not me. Not me. I'm here in Florida. It took Florida to crack the crime cases in New York. That

FBI must be sleeping on the job. The Organized Crime Task Force must be sleeping on the job. The Queens District Attorney must be sleeping on the job. The Brooklyn District Attorney must be sleeping on the job. I was -- all my phones were bugged. My club was bugged, the outside of the club was bugged. There was a video camera in -- on the outside of the club from 2000, I believe -- or 2001 to 2003. I would love to have those papers because if I did, there's no me talking to anybody about committing no crimes or anything else. But, you know, they say like I escaped. What did I escape? I paid my time for my crimes in New York."

"But getting back to why am I here. If the foundation was built with John Gotti and Johnny Alite, I didn't start it. They said that I didn't start it. Why am I here? I don't know. I'm here because if you walk down the street and there's two movie theaters, and one says The Redbook, and the other one says the Redbook is playing here, in this one you got Robert DeNiro, uh, uh, Jack Nicholson and Tom Cruz and in this Redbook you got Mary Quinn, Tom Adams and Larry Smith. What movie are you going to? You're going to that one. I'm the headliner for them. I'm the newspaper maker. I'm going to be their promotion on the way up. Sin, isn't it? And trust me, don't think -- it happens to everybody. It could happen to your son or daughter, your granddaughter or your grandson."

"I seen it. There's nothing this Government will stop at if they want somebody."

UNITED STATES DISTRICT COURT, MIDDLE DISTRICT OF FLORIDA, TAMPA DIVISION, UNITED STATES OF AMERICA, Plaintiff, Case No. 8:04-CR-348-T-24TGW -vs- 18 October 2006, Tampa, Florida. EXCERPT OF TRANSCRIPT OF TRIAL PROCEEDINGS BEFORE THE HONORABLE SUSAN C. BUCKLEW, UNITED STATES DISTRICT COURT JUDGE.

CHAPTER 26

ARY FRANCO and BANGU 2 PRISON in BRAZIL

The Ary Franco Prison in western Rio de Janeiro was condemned by the United Nations. The U.N. Subcommittee on the Prevention of Torture recommended the immediate closure of Ary Franco Prison. It revealed, along with insect and rodent infestation, that human waste from the upper floors were leaking through the floors below. Four hundred and sixty-seven prisoners occupied a space that was origi- nally built for two hundred and ninety-six inmates with thirty men to each thirty-five square meter cell.

Along with the inhumane living conditions, inmate abuse and torture led one of Brazil's justice ministers saying that he "would prefer death to serving time at Ary Franco."

Seven prison guards were accused of torturing forty-six-year-old Chinese-Brazilian businessman Chan Kim Chang, who died after he was found beaten to a pulp with head injuries in a cell at Ary Franco.

The newspaper headlines read:

New York Mafia Street Boss, King of Crime, is Arrested in the

Famous Section of Copacabana, Brazil

ARY FRANCO PRISON, Rio de Janeiro. Everybody in the prison already knew I was coming, and they were expecting me. I was all over the news, the Associated Press, CNN, World News, and they were touting me as one of the most violent street bosses ever captured. Word of mouth in prisons spreads like tidal waves; it always did. It took cuffs and chains, three paddy wagons, and about a dozen fully armed SWAT and military policemen to bring me in.

One of the mistakes I made in getting caught by Interpol happened because I didn't sit still. I didn't sit still because I wasn't sure was what going on back home. No indictment was happening, and the process was taking a long time.

The guards were transporting me from a holding cell to Ary Franco, one of Brazil's worst prisons. When we first pulled in, my initial impression was that the jail looked like an old-style dungeon castle, dark and dreary. I was first taken down into the basement of the jail to what was called "reception." On the inside, it was dark, grey, dirty, and dilapidated. There were huge rats all over the place. I said to myself, "Okay, I'm close to being in fucking Hell, I guess." Because of the notoriety around my case, I had about fifteen intake officers surrounding me. For the normal inmate being processed, there would usually be about six waiting in the basement.

They stripped me down, and then they did what they did to everybody—abused me. In Ary, the abuse was extremely physical. I was handcuffed, and my legs were shackled. I was defenseless as the guards hit, punched, and kicked me.

When their fun was over, I was taken upstairs to the cells. As I was walking through the prison hallway, all the inmates were pressed against the old-style bars of the cell, reaching out with their hands. They spoke in Portuguese, English, and other languages as they yelled out to me. I could only hear clips of sentences through all the noise, "If you need anything—I'm here—"

We stopped in front of the cell where I was going to be assigned. My legs were still shackled, but they had just taken my cuffs off, and that's when one of the guards hit me. Most inmates would've taken the hit and that would've been the end of it, but I swung back. Everyone was screaming, cheering me on because I was fighting back.

That's how it all started. My fighting with the guards enhanced what people had heard about me and my reputation. Everyone saw first-hand how I was going to fight back with aggression. Decades later, some of my former cellmates would speak about our serving time at Ary together, guys like Justin Beck, who did an interview talking about that very fight. "When they gave it to him, he gave it back just as good."

The second those bars were locked behind me, I had already begun scanning and surveying the cell. There were probably about thirty men crammed into a twelve-man cell. Eleven concrete bunks lined the wall, the twelfth one being used like a table.

One wall faced the outside world, and at the top of the ceiling was an opening exposing everyone in the cell to the outside elements. Just outside that opening were armed police who were walking the outside perimeter just above us on a catwalk. I could tell when it was raining because inside the cell, there would be water stains on the sides of the concrete walls.

There were really no lights to speak of, but the guys managed to rig up a light. The problem in these countries was that everyone lost electric on a constant basis because of the poor quality of electricity in the countries. So it wasn't surprising that my first night in Ary would not have any electricity.

I understood right off that I was in a third world country and living in a concentration-camp jail. I didn't dwell on it; I was already in problem-solving mode, looking around and just saying to myself, "How the fuck am I getting out of here?"

Escape is what consumed my mind. How was I going to get out? Who would I have to pay off? What would be the best plan? I wondered if I could convince one of those military policemen to help me.

I studied the catwalk and where it rained inside the cell. I thought if there was a way to cut through those bars, then there was a way out of here. I would be working on that idea in the coming time.

Once a month, we were allowed outside for two hours. The problem was, we were forced to walk naked and barefoot, stepping on rocks and dog shit. The entire field was rocky, surrounded by gun towers, armed guards, and about a dozen guard dogs. We were not allowed to huddle or stand still. We had to keep walking barefoot or be beaten. That was actually a yard rule the warden implemented.

There were other times during shakedowns when we would have to sit outside naked in one spot from seven a.m. till seven p.m. with a hundred military police dressed all in black, wearing masks and holding machine guns on us. They had us sitting naked out in the pouring rain, in one-hundred-twenty-degree weather, the burning sun, the freezing rain, it didn't matter. If one had to shit or piss, they had to do it in the spot they sat in. We weren't allowed to pick up our heads to look around, nor could we look at the guards, or we'd get beat up.

As horrible and vicious as conditions were at Ary Franco Prison, John Alite will tell you that the Bangu 2 Penitentiary Complex was far worse. Bangu is a maximum-security prison comprised of nine penitentiaries and one penal institute. One of the horror-show penitentiaries is the Talavera Bruce, a women's prison. On the complex are four safe houses, a penal sanatorium, and two hospitals.

Fernandinho Beira-Mar, a maniacal Brazilian drug lord, was held in the Bangu 2 Penitentiary Complex from 2001 to 2003 before being transferred to the Presidente Prudente supermax prison near São Paulo.

The most savage and dangerous prisoners were sent to the Bangu 2 Complex. The administration of Ary Franco, having been fed up with John's constant fighting, organizing the inmates, and general chaos, sent John Alite to Bangu.

Over thirty inmates were killed in a riot at Bangu, and a half-dozen prison officials were slaughtered in just a few years.

The Colombian Post did an exposé claiming that almost half the prison guards at Bangu were replaced due to the suspicion that they were being paid by drug traffickers.

Indeed, they were. John Alite, after being held in Bangu for two months, paid a cooperative prison official forty thousand American dollars to be transferred to a private prison, where he planned his escape. Not long after he arrived in the "easy prison," the United States federal officials came for John.

It had been documented; state senators had been quoted, saying they would rather die than have to spend one day at Ary Franco. And here I was, fighting to actually stay here behind these bars as long as possible. Now I just needed to keep my head and stay alive.

Where I lived and was arrested in Brazil

Mafia Royalty

Philadelphia Interview

Interview in Albania

Endorsing assemblywoman from Woodhaven

Albanian Blood!

Albania with my son, far left, Albanian singer Stresi next to him

Good friend, Jason David Frank, The Green Ranger

L-R, Me, Anthony Ruggiano, and Felix Levine

War hero friend, Brian

Me with Lance and Johnny

Guardian Angel, Curtis Sliwa, Geraldo Rivera, and me

Did time with Patrick Jenkins

Albania

Best friend, neurosurgeon Dr. Genti Toshkezi

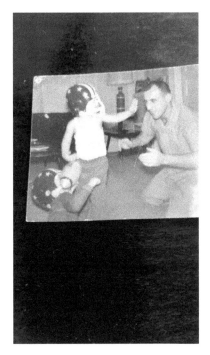

My dad with my brother and me

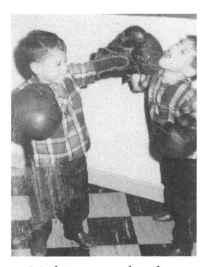

Me hitting my brother

Brazil

Boxing Prince Badi

Bobby Boriello

Me, Camela Gotti at Nancy and Ronnie Trucchio's
daughter, Bliss's christening

Justin Beck and Olu did time with me in UK prison

Cop Phil Barone on far left

Mets player Vince Vaughn with my son, Johnny, and me

Mike, me, Mike Scars

London, Interview with Brazil jail mates

Netflix film, Camden, NJ gym

Prison

Sir Trevor McDonald

Back in Brazil, Claus sitting next to me

West Palm Beach

Gym in Boston

My crew of friends

Albania

Walter Beach III of the Cleveland Browns
We did a talk together

Brazil

Santos Trafficante

My really good friend who was killed, Greg Reiter

Anthony Russo and me

Filming in Sweden with Claus from Denmark

Puerto Rico, after I shot a guy

Anthony, me, Mike in Florida

My dad, far right, his good friend Dino next to him

Me, boxing in Brazil, before being captured

Lightning Source UK Ltd.
Milton Keynes UK
UKHW011846301021
393064UK00003B/7/J